EVERYWHERE IS LOCAL

Recipes and Reflections
to Strengthen Community
and Nurture Well-Being

EVERYWHERE IS LOCAL

Recipes and Reflections
to Strengthen Community
and Nurture Well-Being

ROBYN WRIGHT

Good Food · Good Life

♡

Robyn

Photographs by the author.

Published by

HenschelHAUS Publishing, Inc.

www.henschelhausbooks.com

ISBN: 978159598-743-3

E-ISBN: 978159598-744-0

LCCN: 2019910556

Publisher's Cataloging-In-Publication Data
(Prepared by The Donohue Group, Inc.)
Names: Wright, Robyn, 1967- author, photographer.
Title: Everywhere is local : recipes and reflections to strengthen community and nurture well-being / Robyn Wright.
Description: [Milwaukee, Wisconsin] : HenschelHAUS Publishing, Inc., [2019] | Includes bibliographical references and index.
Identifiers: ISBN 9781595987433 | ISBN 9781595987440 (ebook)
Subjects: LCSH: Cooking (Natural foods) | Local foods. | LCGFT: Cookbooks.
Classification: LCC TX741 .W75 2019 (print) | LCC TX741 (ebook) | DDC 641.563--dc23

Printed in the United States of America.

DEDICATION

To my grandmother, Opal Loveridge Gillilan.

*I miss your apple dumplings and rocking-chair lullabies.
I miss watching you make home-cooked magic that filled
my body and soul with your love.*

*You may not physically be here to hold this book in
your work-worn hands, but please know that those
deeply loved hands influenced every page.*

TABLE OF CONTENTS

A LOVE NOTE TO MY READERS

Hello.

I may not know how this book landed in your hands, but it did, so here we are!

You may love to cook, bake, write menus, and feel passionate about your art and expertise.

I applaud you!

The world needs people like you.

You may feel pretty *meh* about cooking or baking or food prep in general, but something in you would like to explore to see if there might be a few dishes you could fall in love with making.

I applaud you!

The world needs people like you.

You may be a novice out to acquire new skills in a sea of cuisine, and all of this cookbook-reading is like a foreign language.

I applaud you!

The world needs people like you.

When you put food on the table, pack a picnic basket, fill a lunch bag, or share a casserole, you bring something special into existence.

You are a creator.

The world needs people like you.

More than anything, I would love for you to be joyfully present with the recipes in this book. Savor choosing the luscious fruits, vibrant vegetables, and sacred animals that you will be eating. Allow yourself the time and patience to read through directions. Let distractions fall away while you create. Substitute where inspired. Embrace the process.

If the culinary journey is new to you (or not), by all means use the Internet to look up terms that are unfamiliar. Not sure what sauté means? I'm 100% confident you can find a video on the subject. Not familiar with monk fruit? Believe me, a moment of research will pay off.

The genesis of my writing is not to necessarily share new ideas with you, more than it is to share many old ideas wrapped in my own creations. They are foundational ideas to so many open-hearted and creative human beings. And you most certainly are one of them.

Soaking and sprouting grains is not a new idea.

But it may be new to you.

The importance of growing our food in well-nourished, living soil is not a new idea.

But it may be new to you.

The vital need to be an active participant in caring for yourself, each other, and this magnificent planet we share is not a new idea.

But it may be new to you.

All old ideas were once new to someone.

The new idea for me, and the inspiration for writing this book, has been driven by the profuse pleasure I find in knowing and meeting farmers, entrepreneurs, activists, enthusiasts, and epicureans. While I may delight in combining ingredients, it has never been just about the food. It's about the color, the tastes, and the textures, the conversations, the work, the learning, the joy, the seeds, the soil, and the soul.

This book is about finding the words and recipes to connect a light grid of gratitude for all that has brought me to share with you. This book is about introducing you to some special people who commit themselves to making the world a better place through the crops they carefully grow, the animals they lovingly tend to, and the products and experiences that are born from tuning into what makes them feel alive.

I pay homage to them and all like them.

So this book is ultimately about highlighting our interconnection to all and each other. Everywhere is our backyard.

Everywhere is Local.

Love,

ABOUT THE AUTHOR
By Karina Stuke

Forty-three years ago, at the age of nine, Robyn dragged a chair to the kitchen counter of her childhood home. Scampering up to gain a new vantage point, she discovered a spiral-bound cookbook. It's contents contained a collection of cherished recipes shared by members of a church family. Carefully leafing through the pages, Robyn's attention was drawn to a very specific hand-drawn caricature related to one of the recipes. The sketch was that of a devil - complete with pointy horns, a triangular beard, and stark eyes.

The associated recipe? Devil's Food Cake, of course!

Unbeknownst to her, Robyn had stumbled upon the key that unlocked her lifelong gift and passion. Without hesitation (or adult assistance), she followed the instructions and proudly produced the perfect bakery creation. But it wasn't the finished product that lit her young heart on fire; it was the process of creative intention: the patience, presence, and love that went into producing that simple cake.

On that day, a chef was born.

This food journey continued throughout Robyn's youth and young adult years. Prioritizing whole food ingredients while preparing country farm fare with her grandmother, she was exposed to the many secrets seldom revealed in even the most elite of culinary circles. Here she learned the beautiful art of quality food preparation.

Realizing a void in the healthy, reliable convenience food market, Robyn brought life to KalyANa Organics in 2013. These refined sugar-free, gluten-free, organic cooking and baking mixes were made with nutrient-dense almond and coconut flours. In 2014, Robyn was the deserved recipient of Wisconsin's Hottest Kitchen Entrepreneur Award for her KalyANa creations. A judging panel of professional chefs had spoken, and the culinary world was taking notice.

The KalyANa experience opened many new doors for Robyn: additional recipe development, private chef work, increased demands for her diverse menu of cooking classes, and special events catering. Not to mention the meaningful relationships made with adoring fans, as well as committed farmers, health practitioners, and culinary allies in the organic, real food space.

Robyn presents a world of flavor and taste possibilities for the health-conscious, sustainable-minded consumer who is unwilling to sacrifice personal health in the name of enjoying delicious food. Her work is in high demand and highly-regarded in wellness circles, culinary arts groups, and with those who feel a deep responsibility to not just feed their loved ones, but to nourish them.

A lover of travel, Robyn gains inspiration from cultures and communities committed to sustainable, organic, real food movements both domestically and abroad. Time and time again, these priceless experiences reaffirm her belief that everywhere, is indeed, local.

ACKNOWLEDGMENTS

Writing a book, even a cookbook, is harder than I thought and more soul-stretching than I could have ever imagined. The second-guessing, the failed recipes, the cursing, and the self-imposed deadlines all made some days just a wee bit challenging.

Thankfully, my husband, Don Kujawski, walked all those days with me. None of this would have been possible without him and his unequivocal belief and backing, patience, and superior test-recipe-eating abilities. You are the best life-journey, let's-evolve-together partner a girl could ask for. Thank you for standing by me and this project from day one, my dear.

To my daughters, Catherine Wright, Mary Wright-Layton, and Anne Wright, who unfailingly support and inspire me through their intelligence, courage, and convictions. My Catherine Grace, for your insistence years ago, and your persistence still today in enlightenment and clean-eating. Miss Mary, for baking family favorites, for your unabashed appreciation of delicious creations, and for thinking I am a "food genius." To my Anney Girl—your big heart, beautiful baking, and wily wit make my own heart burst with joy. Thank you, my darlings, for making me the woman I am today.

To my sons-in-law Chris Layton, Kris Davidson, and André Blomqvist. Thank you for loving my daughters so well and bringing the gift of boys to my ever-expanding-mother-heart. I can't imagine our family without you.

To my parents, Michael Gillilan and Linda Gauger, for instilling in me the belief that I can accomplish anything. Your love and generosity has allowed me to pursue my dreams. To my step-parents, Wally Gauger and Laura Gillilan, for all the praise and well-wishes along the way.

To my sister, Amber Gillilan Ford, for your listening ear, sensational sense of humor and honest feedback, always. You are a dear friend and I am blessed to have you in my life.

To my life coach, Patty Jackson, who expertly assists me in getting clear and taking inspired action. I am in awe of you. Thank you for being my mentor and friend.

To my publisher, Kira Henschel, for patience and calm in all the minutiae. I appreciate you walking with me through the whole process.

To Karina Stuke, my friend and fabulous fan. Your "About the Author" writing made me want to know myself! Thank you for your bold and beautiful presence in my world. My admiration for you is boundless.

To my large and well-loved circle of friends, for your steadfast encouragement and enfolding safety. Your posts on social media asking "when will it be done?" gave me a boost to keep going when it would have been easy to give up. Your willingness to taste my failures as well as successes is sweet indeed. Your collective light, wisdom, strength and all around super-powers are a glorious force for good in my life and the world at large.

INTRODUCTION

Here are a few thoughts as you dive in or pick some one-off recipes to make.

You will want to have the following tools in your kitchen:

- *immersion blender*
- *stand mixer*
- *electric hand mixer*
- *digital thermometer*
- *food processor*
- *digital scale*
- *dry and liquid measures*
- *mixing bowls*
- *rubber spatula*
- *whisk*
- *mixing spoons*
- *hardwood cutting board*
- *sharp knives*
- *grater*
- *hand juicer*
- *zester*
- *garlic press*
- *tea kettle or electric kettle*
- *parchment paper*
- *good quality cookware*
- *springform pan*
- *rimmed baking sheets*
- *muffin tins*
- *bread pans*
- *2-qt [2-liter] casserole dish*
- *large roasting pan*

All of the recipes in this book are gluten-free. You may see some ingredients you've never heard of before. Try your local, organic grocery store, farmer's market, or internet to collect the items you need. Here is a sample list:

- *almond flour*
- *coconut flour*
- *tapioca or arrowroot flour*
- *sprouted rolled oats*
- *sprouted oat flour*
- *tigernut flour*
- *monk fruit sweetener*
- *coconut sugar*
- *unrefined cane sugar*
- *potato starch*
- *psyllium husk powder*
- *sweet white rice flour*
- *sprouted brown rice flour*
- *nutritional yeast*
- *avocado oil*
- *coconut oil*

Rather than writing "organic," as in "organic butter," "organic broccoli," or "organic tomatoes" a gazillion times; please, please, please assume I intend for all ingredients, or as many as humanly possible, to be organic.

I also intend for any and all meat, eggs, dairy or seafood to be humanely pasture-raised, honorably slaughtered, and/or sustainably wild-caught. With their lives, these precious animals give us life.

When you see "sea salt" in a recipe, please know you may safely substitute with Himalayan pink salt. Please do not use regular table salt. Ever.

Where possible, please use the freshest dried or fresh garden herbs. They make a big difference.

One of the biggest challenges in writing this cookbook for you was selecting the recipes that are in it. I have been collecting and playing with recipes since I was a teenager. Needless to say, there are hundreds of recipes that I like, but they're not in here. I stopped using Cool Whip, Velveeta, margarine, and other food-imposters years ago, so you won't see stuff like that either.

What you will see are mindfully selected recipes that delight the senses and nourish the body. Yes, you will see sweets in here. They are not meant to be a daily occurrence. Sugar really should be consumed sparingly.

With the understanding that many have dietary restrictions and intolerances, I have made substitution suggestions when I tested them. Feel free to modify as desired for your own personal preferences.

And lastly, you will see short bios of some inspiring people scattered throughout these pages. Sharing their brief stories and photos is intended to bring attention to the beauty they bring into the world and provide a feel for the inspiration behind my words and work. They are us, and we are them.

Everywhere is Local

EVERYWHERE IS LOCAL GLUTEN-FREE FLOUR BLEND

This is the gluten-free flour blend I developed for use in my recipes.
Please feel free to use this or another brand of your choice.

INGREDIENTS

- 3½ oz [100 g] psyllium husk powder
- 19¾ oz [560 g] white rice flour or sprouted brown rice flour
- 19¾ oz [560 g] sweet rice flour
- 8½ oz [240 g] tapioca flour
- 8½ oz [240 g] potato starch

Blend all thoroughly and store in an airtight glass jar.

Makes about 14 cups

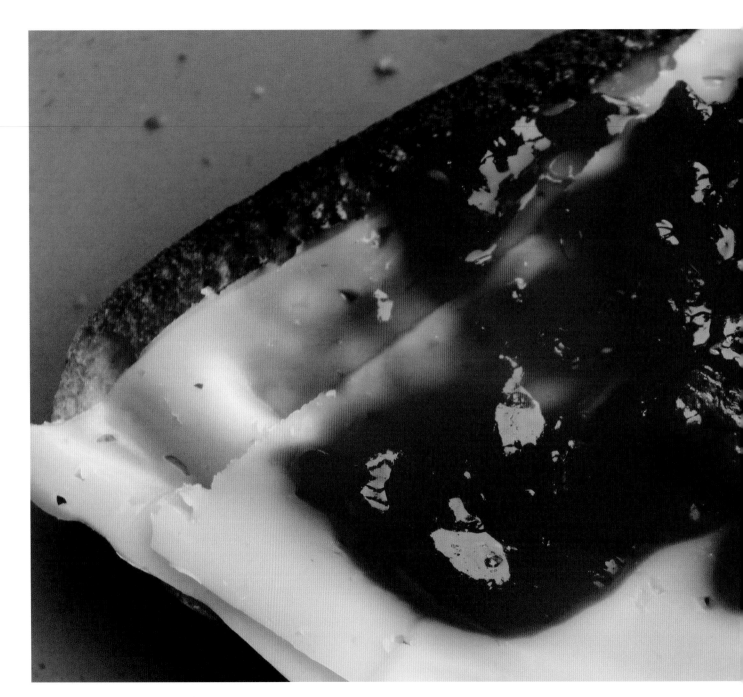

STARTERS & SMALL PLATES

start small
or go big
have an appetizer
for lunch
it's your party
you can cook
what you want to

Pesto Provolone Cake, 9

Manchego Cheese Balls, 11

Sweet & Sassy Chicken Wings, 15

Better-at-Home Crab Cakes, 17

Seeded Rosemary Crackers, 19

Charred Cauliflower with Lemons, Anchovies, & Capers, 21

Butternut-Sage Stuffed Mushrooms, 23

Roasted Smashed Potatoes with Lemon Gremolata, 25

Honey-Drizzled Stuffed Apricots, 27

PESTO PROVOLONE CAKE

Line an 8-cup [2-liter] glass measure or 5-inch [13-cm] diameter bowl (with straight sides) with beeswax cloth, leaving enough overhang to cover the top (or butter generously); set aside.

In the bowl of a food processor, pulse 6 oz [170 g] pine nuts until nearly smooth. Add cream cheese and garlic; pulse until light and fluffy. With an offset or small rubber spatula, spread a few tablespoons of cream cheese mixture onto 7 slices of Provolone cheese. Place the first slice of Provolone cheese (cream-cheese-side up) in the bottom of the prepared glass measure or bowl. Top with one more Provolone slice (cream-cheese-side up). Spread pesto over cream cheese mixture and sprinkle some reserved pine nuts over pesto. Top with another Provolone slice (cream-cheese-side up). Spread with half of the chopped sun-dried tomatoes. Top with the fourth Provolone slice (cream-cheese-side up). Spread more pesto over cream cheese and sprinkle with more pine nuts. Top with the fifth Provolone slice (cream-cheese-side up). Next spread remaining sun-dried tomatoes over cream cheese. Top with the sixth slice of Provolone (cream-cheese-side up). Finish by placing the last Provolone slice with the cream-cheese-side DOWN. Cover the glass measure or bowl and refrigerate at least three hours or freeze for one hour.

Remove from refrigerator and carefully take layered loaf out of glass measure or bowl and place on a serving platter. With remaining whipped cream cheese mixture, frost loaf as desired. Garnish with remaining pine nuts and finely chopped fresh basil. Serve with your favorite crackers.

EnJOY!

INGREDIENTS

- 8 oz [227 g] pine nuts, divided into 6 oz [170 g] and 2 oz [57 g] portions
- 2 8-oz [227 g] cream cheese, room temperature
- 1 teaspoon [10 ml] minced garlic
- 7 slices Provolone cheese
- 3 oz [85 g] oil-packed sun-dried tomatoes, drained, finely chopped and divided
- 3 oz [85 g] prepared or homemade basil pesto
- ¼ oz [7 g] fresh basil leaves, finely chopped

Makes one 5-inch [13-cm] loaf

MANCHEGO CHEESE BALLS

Combine parsley and almonds in a medium bowl; set side. Place cheeses, butter, and cream cheese in the bowl of a food processor. Pulse until well-blended.

Divide cheese mixture in half and form into two balls with hands. Roll each ball in mixture of parsley-almonds. Chill at least one hour.

Serve with crackers, celery or carrot sticks, or thinly sliced baguettes.

EnJOY!

Variation
Omit parsley and almonds and use cheese mixture as a sandwich spread

INGREDIENTS

- ½ cup [120 ml] finely chopped fresh parsley
- 1 cup [240 ml] sliced almonds
- 1 5.2-oz [150 g] Boursin Garlic and Fine Herbs cheese (or alternative)
- 6 oz [170 g] Manchego cheese, finely shredded
- 2 tablespoons [28 g] salted butter, soft
- 4 oz [113 g] cream cheese, soft

Makes two cheese balls

WHELAN'S WILD ROOTS FAMILY FARM
OCONOMOWOC, WISCONSIN

How long do you hold a vision when inspiration hits? Nine days? Nine weeks? Nine moths?

How about nine years? That's what Charles and Gina Whelan did before establishing Whelan's Wild Roots Family Farm in Oconomowoc, Wisconsin.

It all started when starting a family kick-started Charles and Gina into the sustainable food movement. They began making better food choices for their babies and in turn, themselves. The more they learned, the more inspired they became. Gina's growing love for healing herbs began talks of "what would it be like to have a farm?"

Where most of us go house-hunting, the Whelan family started farm-hunting. It was no small task. Farms are not readily available. When they are, they are expensive. Undeterred, the Whelan's listed their house for sale. And waited. And waited. And waited. 18 months later, after much soul-searching, re-evaluating, and doubt-conquering, their house sold. But still no farm to move to.

With only two weeks left in their third short-term rental, and no farm in sight, panic could have easily set in. The frustration of moving with little ones, running an organic hair salon and carpentry business, and the discouragement of two failed farm purchases could have derailed the best of dreams. That's when Gina felt a calm inner-knowing. Something good was going to happen.

She opened an email from her realtor and saw a new listing. It seemed unfeasible for so many reasons. And yet. And yet there was that familiar tug in the heart that led her and Charles to go to the open house. There was a spark of knowing that *this* place felt "at home." That bravery to put it all on the line and write an offer that they knew could easily be rejected. But it wasn't. Not only that, the owners generously invited the Whelen family to move in three months before closing. All this within two weeks. All this with vision-holding, faith and fortitude.

A few years later, after sacrifice, exhaustively hard work, and more determination than they thought possible, the Whelen's are raising pastured heritage breed hogs, chickens, ducks, and beef. They sell their top-quality products to the public as well as to wildly popular restaurants like ID, Braise, Odd Duck, Amilinda, and others.

And this is just the beginning. Gina and Charles are transitioning the farm to a permaculture model where open pollinated pastures of organic corn will have free-ranging hogs and beef cattle, hay paddocks will be grown for animal nutrition and soil health, and medicinal herb gardens will be available to attract pollinators and pick-your-own CSA membership.

A new barn is in the works for culinary herb and flower processing, community events, workshops and farm-stand sales. Chefs from the area are being invited in for future farm dinners. Remodeling, restoration, and renewal drive Gina and Charles forward. Sweat, and sometimes tears, make it happen. With nine-plus years of vision-holding, Whelan's Wild Roots Family Farm is living proof of inspired action and inspiration for all.

EVERYWHERE IS LOCAL

SWEET & SASSY CHICKEN WINGS

In a large glass storage container, whisk together 3 tablespoons [45 ml] honey, avocado oil, sea salt, pepper, black cumin, 1 teaspoon [5 ml] garam masala, paprika, cumin, and rosemary. Add chicken wings, tossing to coat. Cover dish with lid or beeswax cloth. Transfer to refrigerator and let marinate at least 30 minutes or up to overnight.

Preheat oven to 400 F [204 C].

Line a baking sheet with parchment paper and arrange chicken wings in a single layer on parchment paper. Bake for 35 minutes.

Meanwhile, in a small bowl, whisk together remaining 3 tablespoons [45 ml] honey, remaining 1 teaspoon [5 ml] garam masala, and vinegar. Remove wings from oven and brush with honey mixture. Return wings to oven and continue baking until wings are slightly charred and crisp, 15-20 minutes more.

EnJOY!

INGREDIENTS

- ♦ 2 lbs [1 kg] chicken wings
- ♦ 6 tablespoon [90 ml] local honey, divided
- ♦ 3 tablespoons [45 ml] avocado oil
- ♦ 2 teaspoons [10 ml] sea salt
- ♦ 2 teaspoons [10 ml] garam masala, divided
- ♦ ⅛ teaspoon [.6 ml] white or black pepper
- ♦ ¼ teaspoon [1.25 ml] black cumin seed powder (optional)
- ♦ 1 teaspoon [5 ml] paprika
- ♦ ½ teaspoon [2.5 ml] ground cumin
- ♦ 2 teaspoons [10 ml] finely minced fresh rosemary leaves
- ♦ 1 tablespoon [15 ml] apple cider vinegar

Makes 6 servings

BETTER-AT-HOME CRAB CAKES

CRAB CAKES

In a medium bowl, combine crab, panko crumbs, green onions, and parsley; set aside. In a separate medium bowl, whisk together eggs, mayonnaise, lemon juice, dry mustard, Worcestershire sauce, sea salt, and cayenne pepper. Pour egg mixture into crab mixture; stir to combine.

Sprinkle ½ cup [120 ml] panko crumbs on parchment-lined baking sheet. With ¼-cup [60-ml] scoop or dry measure, scoop crab mixture onto crumbs. Sprinkle cakes with remaining ¼ cup [60 ml] crumbs and press in slightly. Chill at least one hour.

Fry cakes in a large frying pan with 3-4 tablespoons [45-60 ml] avocado oil over medium-high heat. Cook cakes in batches to prevent over-crowding. Fry until golden brown, about 3-4 minutes per side. Serve with Remoulade Sauce.

REMOULADE SAUCE

Combine all sauce ingredients except mayonnaise in the bowl of a food processor. Pulse until all is finely chopped. Stir into mayonnaise in a small bowl. Chill until ready to use

EnJOY!

INGREDIENTS

Crab Cakes
♦ 16 oz [454 g] crab meat
♦ 1 cup [240 ml] GF panko breadcrumbs
♦ 2 tablespoons [30 ml] minced fresh parsley
♦ 2 tablespoons [30 ml] minced green onions
♦ 4 pastured eggs
♦ 2 tablespoons [30 ml] mayonnaise
♦ 1 tablespoons [15 ml] fresh lemon juice
♦ 1 teaspoon [5 ml] dry mustard
♦ 2 teaspoons [10 ml] Worcestershire sauce
♦ 1 teaspoon [5 ml] sea salt
♦ ¼ teaspoon [2.5 ml] cayenne pepper
♦ ½ cup [120 ml] GF panko breadcrumbs
♦ Avocado oil for frying

Remoulade Sauce
♦ 1 cup [240 ml] chopped red bell pepper
♦ ¼ cup [60 ml] chopped green onions
♦ ¼ cup [60 ml] Dijon mustard
♦ ¼ cup [60 ml] chopped fresh parsley, packed
♦ ¼ cup [60 ml] local honey
♦ 2 tablespoons [30 ml] chopped shallot
♦ 1 tablespoon [15 ml] fresh lemon juice
♦ ½ teaspoon [2.5 ml] sea salt
♦ 1½-2 cups [360-480 ml] mayonnaise

Makes 12 cakes

SEEDED ROSEMARY CRACKERS

Preheat oven to 300 F [148 C].

Place all ingredients except 2 teaspoons [10 ml] sunflower seeds in the bowl of a food processor. Turn on and grind until all is combined well. Add remaining sunflower seeds and pulse 1-2 times.

Pour dough mixture onto parchment paper cut to fit a baking sheet. Top with a second sheet of same size. Roll dough into a ⅛-inch [30-mm]-thick rectangle; remove top parchment paper.

Using a pizza cutter, score dough into cracker portions.

Bake about 18 to 22 minutes, **rotating pan at the 7-minute mark, and next 7 minute mark until deep golden**. Let cool on rack 15 minutes then carefully break into crackers. Cool completely.

EnJOY!

INGREDIENTS

- 4 oz [113 g] almond flour
- 4 teaspoons [20 ml] raw sprouted sunflower seeds, divided
- 3 tablespoons [45 ml] raw sprouted pumpkin seeds
- 1 teaspoon [5 ml] ground chia-flax blend (I use Nutiva brand)
- ½ teaspoon [2.5 ml] sea salt
- 2 teaspoons [10 ml] olive or avocado oil
- 2 dates, finely chopped or snipped with scissors
- 3 teaspoons [30 ml] fresh rosemary leaves, finely chopped
- 1½ tablespoons [23 ml] water

Makes approximately 20 to 24 crackers

CHARRED CAULIFLOWER WITH LEMON, ANCHOVIES, AND CAPERS

In a small saucepan over medium heat, combine ½ cup [120 ml] olive oil and chopped anchovy fillets; cook slowly until the anchovies begin to dissolve. Add garlic, coriander, marjoram, cayenne pepper, turmeric, and onion powder; cook 1 minute more. Turn off heat and stir in lemon zest and chopped capers; set aside.

Halve and core a large cauliflower and slice florets into 1-inch [2.5 cm] pieces.

Heat a large cast-iron skillet over medium-high heat. Add ¼ cup [60 ml] avocado oil to the pan. Carefully add cauliflower to the hot oil in a single layer. Season with salt and pepper and brown the florets for 4-5 minutes.

With a metal spatula, carefully turn them over and cook for about 2 minutes more, until firm-tender and nicely charred.

Transfer cauliflower to a platter, spoon the anchovy sauce over, and sprinkle with roughly chopped parsley. Serve with lemon wedges.

EnJOY!

INGREDIENTS

- ½ cup [120 ml] olive oil
- 2 oz [56 g] wild caught anchovy fillets, finely chopped
- 2 to 3 garlic cloves, minced
- Pinch coriander
- Pinch marjoram
- Pinch cayenne pepper
- Pinch turmeric
- Pinch onion powder
- Zest from 1 lemon, finely chopped
- 2 tablespoons [30 ml] capers, chopped
- ¼ cup [60 ml] avocado oil
- 1 large cauliflower head
- Salt and freshly ground pepper, to taste
- ¼ cup [60 ml] Italian parsley, chopped
- Lemon wedges for serving

Makes 4 servings

BUTTERNUT-SAGE STUFFED MUSHROOMS

Preheat oven to 375 F [190 C].

Heat oil in a large skillet over medium-high heat. Add butternut squash and cook, stirring occasionally, 8-10 minutes or until tender and browned. Add sage, 1 tablespoon [14 g] butter, sea salt, and pepper; cook, stirring constantly, 2 minutes. Add wine or broth; cook, stirring constantly, 3 minutes. Transfer squash to a medium bowl, and cool about 10 minutes.

Meanwhile, remove and discard mushroom stems; set mushroom caps aside.

Stir goat cheese into squash mixture just until combined.

Melt remaining 2 tablespoons [28 g] butter. In a small bowl, stir breadcrumbs into melted butter just until combined. Spoon desired amount of squash mixture into each mushroom cap. Press about 1 tablespoon [15 ml] breadcrumb mixture onto filling. Place mushrooms in a single layer on a parchment-lined rimmed baking sheet. Bake 15-20 minutes or until breadcrumbs are toasted and golden brown. Sprinkle with chopped fresh parsley when serving (as desired).

EnJOY!

INGREDIENTS

- 12 oz [340 g] butternut squash, peeled and minced (pulse in a food processor)
- 2 tablespoons [30 ml] olive or avocado oil
- 1½ teaspoons [7.5 ml] finely chopped fresh sage leaves
- 3 tablespoons [42 g] salted butter, divided
- ¼ cup [60 ml] dry white wine, vegetable broth, or chicken bone broth
- ½ teaspoon [2.5 ml] sea salt
- ¼ teaspoon [1.25 ml] freshly ground black pepper
- 24 oz [680 g] fresh mushrooms
- 4 oz [113 g] herbed, truffle oil, or plain goat cheese log
- ¼ cup [60 ml] GF panko breadcrumbs or fresh breadcrumbs (from sprouted oat-honey bread)
- Chopped fresh parsley to garnish (optional)

Makes about 12 appetizer servings

ROASTED SMASHED POTATOES
WITH LEMON GREMOLATA

Heat oven to 400 F [204 C]. Line a rimmed baking sheet with parchment paper; set aside.

Boil potatoes in a heavy-bottomed pot just until fork-tender (about 8-10 minutes); drain and place in a large mixing bowl. Add 2 tablespoons [30 ml] avocado oil, garlic, sea salt, and pepper; toss to coat potatoes. Spread potatoes on a lined baking sheet. With the base of a heavy-bottomed glass, gently smash each potato until the insides start to break through. Bake for 25 minutes until golden brown.

While potatoes are baking, fry bacon over medium heat until desired crispness. Remove pan from heat and set aside. In a separate pan over medium heat, melt 2 tablespoons [28 g] butter. When hot, add onions, spreading into an even layer in butter. Allow to cook, undisturbed, for 5 minutes. Remove pan from heat and set aside.

In a small bowl, stir together basil, parsley, lemon zest, and lemon juice. Add sautéed onions, as well as butter drippings from pan; stir well.

Spoon 1 teaspoon [5 ml] basil mixture onto each smashed potato. Top with a sprinkling of cooked bacon pieces including bacon drippings.

EnJOY!

INGREDIENTS

- 1 lb [½ kg] baby potatoes
- 2 tablespoons [30 ml] avocado oil
- 1 to 2 cloves garlic, minced
- ½ teaspoon [2.5 ml] sea salt
- Freshly ground pepper to taste
- 1 cup [240 ml] diced yellow onion (1 medium onion)
- 2 tablespoons [30 ml] butter, ghee, avocado or olive oil
- ¼ cup [60 ml] finely chopped fresh basil leaves
- 2 tablespoons [30 ml] finely chopped Italian parsley
- Zest of 1 lemon
- Juice of 1 lemon
- ½-1 cup [120-240 ml] finely chopped cooked bacon (optional)

Makes 4 to 6 appetizer servings

EVERYWHERE IS LOCAL

HONEY-DRIZZLED STUFFED APRICOTS

DAIRY-FREE OPTION

Place the cashews, lemon juice, nutritional yeast, and salt into the bowl of a food processor. Blend until smooth, stopping to scrape down the sides of the bowl as needed. Add a tablespoon or two of filtered water to thin as needed. Stir in herbs of choice. Divide cashew cheese mixture between apricot halves. Drizzle with honey and top with chopped almonds or pistachios.

DAIRY OPTION

Mix ricotta, cream, and herbs of choice together until well-combined. Divide cheese mixture between apricots halves. Drizzle with honey and top with chopped almonds or pistachios.

EnJOY!

INGREDIENTS

- 8 fresh apricots, halved
- ½ cup [120 ml] chopped sprouted almonds or pistachios
- 2-3 teaspoons [10-15 ml] raw honey

Dairy-free Option
- 1 cup [240 ml] raw cashews, soaked in water 4-8 hours, drained and rinsed
- 1 tablespoon [15 ml] fresh lemon juice
- 1-2 teaspoons [5-10 ml] nutritional yeast
- ¼ teaspoon [1.25 ml] sea salt, or to taste
- 1 to 2 tablespoons [15-30 ml] finely chopped fresh basil, lemon balm, lemon thyme or rosemary

Dairy Option
- 4 oz [113 g] ricotta, room temperature
- 2 teaspoons [10 ml] heavy cream
- 1-2 tablespoons [15-30 ml] finely chopped fresh basil, lemon balm, lemon thyme or rosemary

Makes 8 servings

SOUPS & STEWS

sometimes cleaning out the fridge makes the best soup

Slow-Cooker Butternut Squash Soup, 33

Bone-Broth Vegetable Soup, 35

Scarborough Fair Potato Soup, 37

Garden Tomato-Basil Soup, 39

Gazpacho, 43

Summer Corn & Fish Chowder, 45

Chicken Leek Stew, 47

Slow-Cooker Sprouted Lentil & Sausage Stew, 49

Cream of Mushroom Soup, 51

SLOW-COOKER BUTTERNUT SQUASH SOUP

SOUP

In a 3½- or 4-quart [4-liter] slow cooker, stir together squash, broth, coconut milk, onion, coconut sugar (or sugar of choice), tamari or coconut aminos, fish sauce, and Asian chili sauce.

Cover and cook on low for 4-5 hours or on high for 2-2½ hours. Use an immersion blender to carefully blend soup until completely smooth. (Or, transfer the mixture in batches to a food processor or blender and blend until smooth) Stir in lime juice.

Ladle soup into bowls and top with Cilantro Gremolata. If desired, serve with lime wedges.

CILANTRO GREMOLATA

Toss cilantro, peanuts and lime peel together in a small bowl. Use to garnish each bowl of soup.

EnJOY!

INGREDIENTS

Soup

- 2 pounds [1 kg] butternut squash, peeled and cut into 1-inch pieces
- 2 cups [480 ml] chicken bone broth (or vegetable broth)
- 1 14-oz [397g] can unsweetened full-fat coconut milk
- ¼ cup [60 ml] minced sweet or yellow onion
- 1 tablespoon [15 ml] coconut sugar, date sugar or brown sugar
- 2 tablespoons [30 ml] fish sauce
- 2 tablespoons [30 ml] tamari sauce or coconut aminos
- ½ to 1 teaspoon [2.5-5 ml] Asian chili sauce (sriracha)
- 4 tablespoons [60 ml] fresh lime juice
- 1 recipe Cilantro Gremolata (see below)
- Lime wedges (optional)

Cilantro Gremolata

- ½ cup [120 ml] chopped fresh cilantro or Thai basil
- ½ cup [120 ml] chopped dry-roasted peanuts
- 1 tablespoon [15 ml] finely shredded lime peel

Makes 4 to 6 servings

BONE-BROTH VEGETABLE SOUP

If using beef, sauté in a large pot in avocado oil on medium-high heat until all sides are brown. Remove from oil and set aside on a plate.

In the same pot, heat butter (or avocado oil) over medium heat. Add onions and 3 teaspoons [15 ml] sea salt and sauté until onions are translucent, 5-10 minutes. Add carrots, celery, turnips (and/or beets), potatoes, and cabbage. Stir in beef stew meat (if using). Stir and cook 5-10 minutes more. Pour in bone broth; bring to boil, reduce heat, cover, and simmer 1 hour.

Add remaining ingredients, bring back to boil, cover pan, and simmer an additional 30 minutes until beef and vegetables are fork-tender.

Adjust seasonings to taste.

EnJOY!

INGREDIENTS

♦ 1 lb [454 g] pastured beef stew meat, cut into bite-sized pieces (optional)

♦ 4 tablespoons [60 ml] avocado oil (if using beef)

♦ 4 tablespoons [57 g] pastured butter (or 60 ml avocado oil)

♦ 6 oz [170 g] peeled and diced turnips (or beets or combination of the two)

♦ 1 lb [454 g] diced yellow potato

♦ 6 oz [170 g] chopped yellow or white onion

♦ 8 oz [227 g] carrot, scrubbed and chopped

♦ 2 oz [57 g] celery, sliced

♦ 1 lb [454 g] chopped green cabbage

♦ 6 cups [1.5 liters] bone broth of choice (or rich vegetable broth)

♦ 18 oz [510 g] whole, peeled tomato puree

♦ 1 tablespoon [15 ml] cider vinegar

♦ 1 tablespoon [15 ml] raw honey

♦ ½ oz [14 g] fresh parsley, chopped

♦ 1 teaspoon [5 ml] dried summer savory

♦ 1 teaspoon [5 ml] dried thyme leaves

♦ 3 teaspoons [15 ml] sea salt

♦ ½ teaspoon [2.5 ml] freshly ground black pepper or black cumin seed powder

Makes 4 to 6 servings

SCARBOROUGH FAIR POTATO SOUP

Melt the butter (and bacon fat, if using) over medium heat in a large soup pot. Add the leek, kale, and garlic. Cook, stirring occasionally, until soft and wilted, about 10 minutes.

Add the potatoes, broth, sage, rosemary, thyme, sea salt, and pepper to pot; bring to a boil. Cover and turn the heat to low. Simmer for 15-20 minutes, or until the potatoes are very soft.

Purée the soup with an immersion blender until smooth or transfer to a blender with care and blend until smooth; returning to pot. Add the heavy cream (or milk of choice) and bring to a simmer. Taste and adjust seasonings to your preference. If soup is too thin, simmer further until desired thickness. If it is too thick, add water or broth to thin for desired consistency.

Garnish with fresh parsley and cooked bacon (as desired).

EnJOY!

INGREDIENTS

- ♦ 4 tablespoons [56 g] pastured butter or ghee, or olive oil [60 ml]
- ♦ 1 tablespoon [15 ml] bacon fat (optional, but fabulous)
- ♦ 4 large leeks, white and light green parts only, chopped
- ♦ 3 cloves garlic, peeled and minced
- ♦ 3 oz [85 g] (8 to 10) kale leaves (your choice of variety), de-stemmed and chopped
- ♦ 2 lbs [1 kg] yellow potatoes (peeling optional), chopped into ½-inch [13 mm] pieces
- ♦ 6 cups [1.5 liters] vegetable stock or chicken bone broth
- ♦ 1 cup [240 ml] heavy cream or milk of choice
- ♦ 8 fresh sage leaves, chopped
- ♦ 3 springs fresh rosemary, de-stemmed and leaves chopped
- ♦ 4 springs fresh thyme, leaves removed
- ♦ 1½ teaspoons [7.5 ml] sea salt
- ♦ ½ teaspoon [2.5 ml] freshly ground black pepper or black cumin seed powder
- ♦ 3 springs fresh parsley, chopped, reserved
- ♦ 3 slices bacon, chopped and fried for garnish (optional-but fabulous)

Makes 6 servings

GARDEN TOMATO-BASIL SOUP

Heat the olive or avocado oil in a large, heavy-bottomed pot over medium-low heat. Add the onions and carrots; sauté about 10 minutes, until carrots are tender. Add the garlic and cook for 1-2 minutes more.

Add tomatoes, honey (or sugar of choice), tomato paste, basil, oregano, vegetable or chicken broth, vinegar or lemon juice, salt and pepper; stirring well. Raise heat to medium-high until boiling. Once boiling, reduce heat to low and simmer 30-40 minutes.

Stir in cream (or coconut milk). Purée with an immersion blender until smooth. Add butter or ghee (if desired). Garnish with finely chopped basil leaves.

EnJOY!

INGREDIENTS

- ¼ cup [60 ml] olive or avocado oil
- 1½ cups [360 ml] chopped red or yellow onions
- 2 carrots, scrubbed and chopped
- 3 cloves fresh garlic, minced
- 4 lbs [1.8 kg] tomatoes, peeled, seeded and chopped (see directions in Gazpacho recipe)
- 1 teaspoon [5 ml] raw honey, coconut sugar or brown sugar
- 2 tablespoons [30 ml] tomato paste
- ¼ cup [60 ml] chopped fresh basil leaves
- 2 teaspoons [10 ml] chopped fresh oregano leaves
- 3 cups [720 ml] vegetable or chicken broth
- 1 tablespoon [15 ml] apple cider vinegar or fresh lemon juice
- 1 tablespoon [15 ml] sea salt
- 2 teaspoons [10 ml] freshly ground black pepper
- ¾ cup [80 ml] heavy cream or full-fat coconut milk
- 3 tablespoons [42 g] pastured butter or ghee (optional, but delicious)
- Fresh basil (for garnish)

Makes 4 to 6 servings

LOS PERROS URBAN FARM, MALMÖ, SWEDEN

Who would have imagined that Sofia Reuterving, from Sweden, and Buddha Browett, from Australia, would grow up, meet in Barcelona, and eventually start one of the first and largest commercial urban farms in Sweden? Well, it happened, and Malmö, Sweden will be forever changed because of their vision, hard work, and perseverance.

Since the Spring of 2015, Los Perros Urban Farm has grown to 2500 square meters of sustainably cultivated crops. Using only hand tools, manure, compost and huge commitment, Sofia and Buddha deliver a large variety of pesticide-free vegetables to restaurants and the local community via bicycle! That's seed-to-table green and an inspiration to all small-scale farmers everywhere!

Los Perros Urban Farm was instrumental in creating Reko-Ring Malmö. Reko-Ring is a FaceBook group where local food growers and producers put out weekly ads with weekly harvest and product information, and community members order and pick everything up at a set time and place directly from their farmer. It's an ingenious online farmer's market!

If their farm was not enough, Buddha and Sofia put more work and love into Flax—a sustainable cafe, workshop and farm stand in Malmö. Their dedication to walking the talk will undoubtedly have a ripple effect in Sweden and beyond!

GAZPACHO

Fill a 6-quart [6-liter] pot halfway full of water, set over high heat, and bring to boil.

Make an "X" with a paring knife on the bottom of each tomato. Slide the tomatoes into the boiling water and set timer for 30-45 seconds. Remove tomatoes to an ice bath (large bowl filled with ice and cold water) and allow to cool, approximately 1-2 minutes. Peel and core the tomatoes. Next, seed the tomatoes, using your fingers, into a fine mesh strainer set over a bowl or glass measure to catch the juice. Press as much of the juice through the strainer as possible.

Combine strained juice with 1 cup [240 ml] bottled tomato juice along with tomatoes in a large mixing bowl. Add cucumber, sweet red pepper, onion, garlic (if using), olive oil, lime juice, lemon juice, balsamic vinegar, Worcestershire, cumin, sea salt, and pepper; stir. Transfer 1½ cups [360 ml] of the mixture to a blender and purée for 15-20 seconds on high speed OR transfer 1½ cups [360 ml] mixture to a 2-cup [480-ml] glass measure and use an immersion blender to purée. Return the puréed mixture to the bowl and stir to combine.

Cover and chill for 2 hours or up to overnight. Garnish with fresh basil.

EnJOY!

INGREDIENTS

- 1½ lbs [680 g] garden-fresh tomatoes, peeled, seeded, and diced (see instructions)
- 1 cup [240 ml] bottled tomato juice
- 1 cup [240 ml] peeled, seeded and diced cucumber
- ½ cup [120 ml] diced sweet red pepper
- ½ cup [120 ml] diced sweet onion
- 1 garlic clove, minced (optional)
- ¼ cup [60 ml] extra-virgin olive oil
- 1 lime, juiced
- 1 lemon, juiced
- 1 tablespoon [15 ml] balsamic vinegar
- 1 tablespoon [15ml] Worcestershire sauce
- ½ teaspoon [2.5 ml] ground cumin
- 1 teaspoon [5 ml] sea salt
- ¼ teaspoon [1.25 ml] freshly ground black pepper
- 2 tablespoons [30 ml] finely sliced fresh basil leaves
- Ice

Makes 4 servings

EVERYWHERE IS LOCAL

SUMMER CORN AND FISH CHOWDER

In a large soup pot, melt butter over medium heat and add corn, red potatoes, celery and onion. Sauté 10 minutes, stirring occasionally.

Add bone broth and fish filets to vegetables in soup pot, turn heat to medium-high and bring to boil. Once boiling, reduce heat to medium-low, cover and simmer 10 minutes.

Test potatoes for doneness (they should be fork-tender). Fish should be opaque and flake easily with fork. Using fork, break fish into chunks.

Stir in cream and seasonings. Salt to taste. Simmer on low heat an additional 5 minutes.

EnJOY!

INGREDIENTS

- 4 ears fresh corn, kernels cut off cob
- 4 medium red potatoes, diced
- 6 stalks celery, diced
- 1 large yellow onion, diced
- ½ cup [113 g] pastured butter or ghee
- 2 large cod or halibut filets (approximately 24 oz [680 g])
- 28-32 oz [1 liter] chicken bone broth
- 2 cups [480 ml] heavy cream
- 4 tablespoons [60 ml] chopped fresh parsley
- 2 teaspoons [10 ml] minced fresh thyme or lemon thyme (my favorite)
- ¼ teaspoon [1.25 ml] white pepper
- ⅛ teaspoon [.6 ml] paprika
- ⅛ teaspoon [.6 ml] dry mustard powder
- Sea salt to taste

Makes 4 to 6 servings

CHICKEN LEEK STEW

Heat a large soup pot over medium heat; add the butter and avocado oil. While butter is melting, in a shallow bowl, blend rice flour, paprika, herbs de Provence, and sea salt. Dredge chicken thighs in rice flour mixture, reserving remaining flour. Carefully place thighs in hot butter-oil and fry, 5 minutes per side until golden. Remove chicken from pot; set aside.

Add onions, leeks, carrots, potatoes and celery to pot. Sauté, stirring occasionally for 5 minutes. Add minced fresh garlic and black pepper. Sauté an additional 3 minutes.

Sprinkle reserved rice flour mixture over vegetables in pot. Stir to combine. Cook 1 minute more. Pour in chicken bone broth and stir until broth bubbles and thickens. Add thyme, rosemary springs, and reserved chicken thighs.

Cover and reduce heat to low. Simmer 1 hour until the chicken thighs are cooked through and a meat thermometer reads 165 F [74 C]. Remove thyme and rosemary sprigs.

EnJOY!

INGREDIENTS

- ◆ 4 organic pastured chicken thighs
- ◆ ¼ cup [60 ml] white rice flour
- ◆ ½ teaspoon [2.5 ml] paprika
- ◆ 1 teaspoon [5 ml] herbs de Provence
- ◆ 1 teaspoon [5 ml] sea salt
- ◆ 5 tablespoons [80 g] pastured butter
- ◆ 1 tablespoon [15 ml] olive or avocado oil
- ◆ 2 medium leeks, white and light green parts of the stem cut in half and chopped diagonally ¼-inch [6 mm] thick
- ◆ 1 medium yellow onion, chopped
- ◆ 4 medium celery stalks, chopped diagonally ¼-inch [6 mm] thick
- ◆ 4 medium carrots, chopped ¼-inch [6 mm] thick
- ◆ 3 medium Yukon gold potatoes, cut into ½-inch [13 mm] cubes
- ◆ 2 cloves of garlic, finely chopped
- ◆ ½ teaspoon [2.5 ml] freshly ground black pepper
- ◆ 14-16 oz [475 ml] chicken bone broth (for soup: 28 to 32 oz [1 liter] chicken bone broth)
- ◆ 3 fresh thyme sprigs
- ◆ 3 fresh rosemary sprigs

Makes 4 servings

SLOW-COOKER SPROUTED LENTIL AND SAUSAGE SOUP

Rinse and drain lentils and rice.

Place all ingredients in a slow cooker.

Cook on low setting for 6 hours, stirring occasionally.

Adjust seasonings according to taste.

EnJOY!

INGREDIENTS

- 1 cup [240 ml] uncooked, sprouted lentils
- ½ cup [120 ml] uncooked, sprouted brown or white rice
- ½ lb [225 g] kielbasa, bratwurst, or other sausage of choice, cut into ½-inch pieces
- 1 cup [240 ml] diced yellow onion
- 1 cup [240 ml] scrubbed and diced carrot
- 1 cup [240 ml] diced celery
- 1 cup [240 ml] diced potato (I keep skins on—your preference)
- 6 cups [1.5 liters] beef bone broth
- 2 tablespoons [30 ml] chopped, fresh parsley
- 1 tablespoon [15 ml] chopped fresh marjoram or oregano
- 1 teaspoon [5 ml] sea salt
- ½ teaspoon [2.5 ml] fresh ground black pepper
- ½ teaspoon [2.5 ml] sweet or smoked paprika
- ½ teaspoon [2.5 ml] garlic salt
- ⅛ teaspoon [.6 ml] ground nutmeg
- ¼ teaspoon [1.25 ml] cayenne pepper (optional)

Makes 6 to 8 servings

CREAM OF MUSHROOM SOUP

Melt butter (or ghee or coconut oil) in large pot over medium heat. Add the mushrooms, onion and garlic; cook until onions are soft.

Pour in the chicken bone broth (or vegetable stock), add the summer savory (if using), paprika, nutmeg, and thyme leaves to the soup. Season to taste, cover and simmer 15-20 minutes.

Pour in the cream (or milk of choice) and remove from heat. Remove 2 cups [480 ml] soup to glass measure and puree with immersion blender. Return puree to pot and stir.

Ladle soup into bowls and drizzle with truffle oil (as desired).

EnJOY!

INGREDIENTS

- 4 tablespoons [56 g] pastured butter, ghee or 60 ml coconut oil
- 4 cups [1 liter] mushrooms of choice, sliced
- 1 yellow onion, diced
- 2 garlic cloves, minced
- 2 cups [480 ml] vegetable stock or chicken bone broth
- 4 sprigs fresh thyme (or lemon thyme), leaves removed
- ½ cup [120 ml] collagen powder (optional)
- ¾ cup [180 ml] cream, cashew milk or full-fat coconut milk
- ½ teaspoon [2.5 ml] summer savory (optional)
- ½ teaspoon [2.5 ml] paprika
- ¼ teaspoon [1.25 ml] nutmeg
- Sea salt and freshly ground black pepper
- Truffle oil (optional, and delicious)

Makes 4 servings

SALADS

toss it
compose it
dress it
enjoy it

Blackberry Blood Orange Salad, 57

Wild Shrimp Mediterranean Salad, 59

Family Potato Salad, 61

Caesar Salad, 65

Almond Cabbage Chicken Salad, 67

French Red Potato Salad, 69

Summer Corn Salad, 71

Blueberry-Beet Salad, 73

Apple Walnut Harvest Salad, 75

BLACKBERRY-BLOOD ORANGE SALAD

VINAIGRETTE

Zest blood orange before juicing. With wire whisk or immersion blender, emulsify vinegar, oil and orange juice. Stir in remaining ingredients. Set aside.

SALAD

Layer lettuce, oranges, blackberries, pistachios, mint leaves, and chèvre on a large platter. Drizzle with blood orange vinaigrette.

EnJOY!

INGREDIENTS

Vinaigrette

- 2 tablespoons [30 ml] raw apple cider vinegar
- ¼ cup [60 ml] avocado oil
- Juice of 1 blood orange (or orange of choice)
- Zest of 1 blood orange (or orange of choice), finely chopped
- 2 tablespoons [30 ml] finely chopped fresh mint leaves
- 1 tablespoon [15 ml] raw, local honey
- ¼ teaspoon [1.25 ml] sea salt
- ⅛ teaspoon [.6 ml] fresh ground black pepper

Salad

- 8 cups [2 liters] torn red leaf lettuce (or romaine)
- 2 blood oranges (or oranges of choice), peeled and chopped
- 8 oz [226 g] blackberries
- ½ cup [120 ml] finely chopped pistachios
- ¼ cup [60 ml] finely chopped fresh mint leaves
- 2 oz [60 g] chevre, crumbled

Makes 4 servings

WILD SHRIMP MEDITERRANEAN SALAD

Combine **Shrimp Marinade** ingredients in a 1-cup [240-ml] glass measure and pour over shrimp in 9-inch [23–cm] glass pie plate or 2-quart [2-liter] casserole. Allow to marinate no more than 30 minutes. Bake shrimp in marinade at 400 F for 8-10 minutes.

Combine **Mediterranean Vinaigrette** ingredients in a 1-cup [240 ml] glass measure, set aside.

Arrange, layer, or toss romaine lettuce, tomatoes, cucumber, bell pepper, onion, parsley, olives, feta cheese, and cooked shrimp on a large serving platter. Drizzle with vinaigrette as desired.

EnJOY!

Salad

- 10 ounces [284 g] chopped romaine lettuce (about 2 medium heads)
- 2 cups [480 ml] cherry tomatoes or heirloom variety, chopped
- 1 small English cucumber, chopped
- 1 red or orange sweet bell pepper, chopped
- ½ medium red onion, finely diced
- ½ cup [120 ml] chopped fresh Italian parsley
- ½ cup [120 ml] pitted Kalamata olives, halved
- 6 ounces [170 g] feta cheese, sliced into ¼-inch [6 mm] cubes or crumbled
- 1 lb [454 g] uncooked wild-caught shrimp, peeled and rinsed

INGREDIENTS

Shrimp Marinade

- ¼ cup [60 ml] olive oil
- ¼ cup [60 ml] fresh lemon juice
- 3 garlic cloves, finely minced
- 1 teaspoon [5 ml] sea salt
- ¼ teaspoon [1.25 ml] freshly ground black pepper
- 2 teaspoons [10 ml] raw local honey
- 1 tablespoon [15 ml] fresh lemon thyme leaves
- 1 teaspoon [5 ml] smoked paprika or Za'atar spice blend

Mediterranean Vinaigrette

- ½ cup [240 ml] olive oil
- Juice of 2 lemons
- ¼ cup [60 ml] chopped fresh parsley or lemon thyme leaves (or combination)
- 1 tablespoon [15 ml] fresh chopped oregano leaves (or 1 teaspoon [5 ml] dried oregano)
- ½ teaspoon [2.5 ml] sea salt
- ⅛ teaspoon [.6 ml] freshly ground black pepper
- 2 cloves garlic, finely minced or pressed
- 2 teaspoons [10 ml] raw local honey
- ½ teaspoon [2.5 ml] Za'atar spice blend (optional)

Makes 4 servings

FAMILY POTATO SALAD

Inspired by Grandma and a family favorite!

Bring potatoes to a boil in a large pot of cold, salted water over high heat. Once boiling, turn heat to medium-high for a lightly rolling boil and boil 15-20 minutes or until potatoes are fork-tender. Drain water and place potatoes in an ice water bath for 2-3 minutes. Pour off ice water and allow potatoes to cool in a colander.

Once potatoes are cool enough to handle, peel skins and cut into ½-inch chunks (or preferred size pieces) and place in a large bowl. Stir in chopped eggs, onion, pickles, celery, and fresh dill. In a large glass measure or medium bowl, combine vinegar, pickle juice, mayonnaise, cream, mustard, sugar (or honey), sea salt, and pepper. Pour mayonnaise sauce over potato mixture in bowl. Adjust sea salt and pepper to taste. If you like your salad to be saucier, add more mayonnaise as desired.

If using, slice reserved hard boiled eggs and place on top of salad. Sprinkle all with paprika and chives. Chill at least 2 hours before serving.

EnJOY!

INGREDIENTS

- 2 lbs [1 kg] Yukon Gold or white potatoes
- 8 hard-boiled eggs, peeled and chopped, reserving 1-2 eggs for slicing on top of salad if desired
- ½ yellow onion, finely diced
- ¼ cup [60 ml] dill pickles, diced
- 2 celery stalks including leaves, diced
- 2 tablespoons [30 ml] finely chopped fresh dill
- 1 tablespoon [15 ml] apple cider vinegar
- 2 tablespoons [30 ml] dill pickle juice
- 1½ cups [360 ml] mayonnaise
- ¼ cup [60 ml] heavy cream
- 2 tablespoons [30 ml] yellow mustard
- 2 teaspoons [10 ml] sugar or raw honey
- 2 teaspoons [10 ml] sea salt
- 1 teaspoon [5 ml] black pepper
- 2 tablespoons [30 ml] fresh chives, finely chopped
- Paprika
- Ice water bath

Makes 4 to 6 servings

STONE BANK FARM MARKET
STONE BANK, WISCONSIN

Know Your Farmer, Know Your Food. It may be the tag line for Stone Bank Farm Market's forward face to the world, but it is also the heart-and-soul vision of the market's lead farmer, Kim Roncone.

At the age of five, helping Grandpa dig up potatoes, pick peppers, and tend to the family garden left an indelible love-memory. Later in life, while working for the Girl Scouts, Kim's father passed away. This led to self-reflective questions. Though she loved the Girl Scouts, there was a bigger "What am I doing?" question that led her in a new direction.

With a passion for growing vegetables and teaching gardening skills to her community, she started small. And as with many great things that start small, the gardens and expertise grew. Stone Bank Farm Market is Kim's first commercial farm enterprise and she cannot imagine doing or loving anything more.

Kim holds a big vision for Stone Bank Farm Market. This includes educating the community on how healthy food is grown and so much more. She told me, "When we can bring a young child to the farm so they experience lettuce just harvested or learn how toxic-free food is grown, that can be life-changing. Customers can see the progress of the growing season and enjoy seasonal eating. We can support other farms and artisans in the market. We offer classes to learn raised-bed gardening and how to extend the growing season. Local chefs and talented teachers offer cooking classes and farm-to-table dinners. We have yoga in the barn and pizza nights in the summer"

Kim especially loves "Kids on the Farm." This program invites kindergarten group visits, playing in the soil, cooking, and hands-on-learning. It is about cultivating appreciation for the food and farmers in our area to bridge the disconnect between how food is grown and what we eat at the table. Kim hopes that these experiences influence their little visitors into adulthood.

If she could wave a magic wand, you would see pastured beef and poultry, an orchard, asparagus, rhubarb and bees at Stone Bank Farm Market. It would look like the old-fashioned farm that conjures nostalgia and fond feelings. With the help of her hard-working mother (Barb), assistant (Danica), and loyal volunteers, wand-waving-Kim could truly manifest more real magic for the surrounding community in the not-too-distant future!

CAESAR SALAD

In a small bowl or 2-cup [480 ml] glass measure, whisk together the garlic, anchovies (include olive oil as desired), lemon juice, Dijon mustard, and Worcestershire sauce. Add the mayonnaise, Parmesan, sea salt, and pepper, and whisk until well combined. Taste and adjust to your liking.

In a large bowl, toss together the salad ingredients. Spoon desired amount of dressing onto salad (this dressing recipe makes more than enough). Toss salad and dressing together.

EnJOY!

INGREDIENTS

Dressing

- 2 small garlic cloves, minced
- 1.5 oz [43 g] jar wild-caught flat anchovy fillets in pure olive oil-minced and smashed
- Juice of 1 lemon
- 1 teaspoon [5 ml] Dijon mustard
- 1 teaspoon [5 ml] Worcestershire sauce
- 1 cup [240 ml] mayonnaise
- ½ cup [120 ml] freshly grated parmesan cheese
- ¼ teaspoon [1.25 ml] sea salt
- ¼ teaspoon [1.25 ml] freshly ground black pepper

Salad

- 2 heads of romaine lettuce, chopped
- 1 cup [240 ml] shaved Parmesan or Asiago cheese
- 1 cup [240 ml] sliced almonds
- sliced or chopped tomatoes (optional)

Makes 4 to 6 servings

ALMOND-CABBAGE [CHICKEN] SALAD

In a small bowl or glass measure, emulsify brown rice vinegar, lemon juice, and sesame oil with an immersion blender (or use a high-speed blender cup). Whisk in remaining dressing ingredients.

In a large bowl, combine salad ingredients. Pour dressing over all; toss well. Garnish with additional cilantro as desired.

EnJOY!

INGREDIENTS

Salad

- 8 oz [227 g] finely sliced Savoy or Nappa cabbage
- 4 oz [115 g] finely sliced purple (red) cabbage
- 1 oz [28 g] fresh cilantro leaves, roughly chopped
- 3 oz [85 g] sliced almonds or chopped sprouted almonds
- 2 tablespoons [30 ml] black and tan gomasio (or plain black or white sesame seeds)
- 4 green onions, finely chopped
- 8 oz [227 g] chopped cooked chicken (optional)

Dressing

- ¼ cup [60 ml] brown rice vinegar
- Juice of 2 fresh lemons
- ½ cup [120 ml] sesame oil
- 1 tablespoon [15 ml] tamari or coconut aminos
- 1 tablespoon [15 ml] pure maple syrup or brown sugar
- ½ teaspoon [2.5 ml] ground black cumin seed or black pepper

Makes 4 servings

FRENCH RED POTATO SALAD

Place potatoes in a large saucepan. Cover with cold water and add 2 tablespoons [30 ml] sea salt. Bring potatoes to boil over high heat, reduce heat to medium and simmer until potatoes are just tender, 5-10 minutes. Remove from heat, drain off hot water and put potatoes in large ice water bath. Set aside until potatoes are cool. Drain off water.

Meanwhile, in a small bowl or glass measure, emulsify avocado or olive oil with champagne vinegar and vermouth (if using) with an immersion blender (or use a high-speed blender cup). Whisk in remaining vinaigrette ingredients.

In a large bowl, combine potatoes, capers, and shallots. Drizzle vinaigrette over all; toss. Chill or serve at room temperature.

EnJOY!

INGREDIENTS

Salad

- 2 lbs [1 kg] red potatoes, quartered and sliced ¼-inch [60mm] thick
- 2 tablespoons [30 ml] sea salt
- Large ice water bath
- 1 tablespoon [15 ml] capers, finely chopped
- 1 shallot, finely chopped

Vinaigrette

- ⅔ cup [158 ml] avocado or extra-virgin olive oil
- ¼ cup [60 ml] champagne vinegar or white wine vinegar
- 2 tablespoons [30 ml] dry vermouth (optional)
- ¼ cup [60 ml] stone ground honey Dijon mustard
- 1 teaspoon [5 ml] sea salt
- 3 tablespoons [45 ml] chopped fresh parsley leaves
- 2 tablespoons [30 ml] chopped fresh chives
- 1 tablespoon [15 ml] chopped fresh tarragon leaves

Makes 6 servings

SUMMER CORN SALAD

For the dressing, in a glass bowl or 2-cup [480-ml] glass measure, whisk together oil, vinegar, lemon juice, sugar or honey, sea salt, and black pepper until sugar or honey is dissolved. Let dressing stand while preparing salad.

For salad, in a large bowl, toss corn and remaining ingredients except arugula leaves or lettuce.

To serve, transfer salad to large serving bowl. Season with the ½ teaspoon [2.5 ml] sea salt. Add the dressing and gently toss in arugula leaves or lettuce. Serve immediately.

EnJOY!

INGREDIENTS

Dressing

- ¼ cup [60 ml] olive oil
- ¼ cup [60 ml] raw apple cider vinegar
- ¼ cup [60 ml] fresh lemon juice
- ¼ cup [60 ml] cane, date or coconut sugar or raw local honey
- 1 teaspoon [5 ml] sea salt
- ½ teaspoon [2.5 ml] freshly ground black pepper

Salad

- 4 ears fresh corn, (blanched 30 seconds if desired), kernels cut from cob
- ½ cup [120 ml] finely diced red onion, soaked in ice water 20 minutes, drained and patted dry
- ½ cup [120 ml] English cucumber or regular cucumber (seeded and peeled), diced or finely sliced
- ½ cup [120 ml] finely diced sweet red pepper
- ½ cup [120 ml] cherry or pear tomatoes, halved or heirloom tomatoes, seeded and chopped
- ¼ cup [60 ml] chopped fresh parsley or cilantro
- 2 tablespoons [30 ml] chopped fresh basil
- 1 tablespoon [15 ml] finely minced, seeded jalapeño
- 2 cups [480 ml] baby arugula leaves or baby mixed lettuces
- ½ teaspoon [2.5 ml] sea salt

Makes 4 to 8 servings

EVERYWHERE IS LOCAL

BLUEBERRY-BEET SALAD

ROAST THE BEETS

Preheat oven to 400 F [204 C]. Using a sharp vegetable peeler, remove the skin from the beets and chop them into ½-inch [2.5 cm] pieces. Wrap the beet pieces in a piece of parchment paper, followed by a piece of aluminum foil to make a sealed packet. Roast beets in their packet on a baking sheet for 45-60 minutes, or until soft. Allow to cool.

PREPARE THE DRESSING

While the beets are cooling, prepare dressing. In a blender or glass container with an immersion blender, blend all the ingredients together except the fresh herbs (if using). Stir in herbs (optional). Taste and adjust seasoning, adding more honey as desired.

ASSEMBLE SALAD

Divide the greens between four plates. Sprinkle each plate with one quarter of the beets, one quarter of the blueberries, one quarter of the cheese. Sprinkle chopped pistachios over all. Drizzle with salad dressing or serve on the side.

EnJOY!

INGREDIENTS

Salad

- 8 cups [2 liters] fresh mixed greens
- 8 oz [226 g] roasted beets
- 8 oz [226 g] fresh blueberries
- 4 oz [113 g] grated raw goat milk cheddar
- 4 oz [113 g] pistachios or almonds, coarsely chopped

Dressing

- 6 oz [170 g] fresh blueberries
- ½ cup [120 ml] balsamic vinegar
- ½ cup [120 ml] olive or avocado oil
- 1 tablespoon [15 ml] Dijon mustard
- 1 tablespoon [15 ml] local honey
- ½ teaspoon [2.5 ml] sea salt
- ¼ teaspoon [1.25 ml] fresh black pepper
- 1 teaspoon [5 ml] lavender buds or finely chopped fresh rosemary (optional)

Makes 4 servings

EVERYWHERE IS LOCAL

APPLE WALNUT HARVEST SALAD

DRESSING

Place vinegar, onion, pure maple syrup, sea salt, and mustard in blender. While processing, gradually add oil in a steady stream. Transfer to a glass measure; stir in poppy seeds.

SALAD

Toss lettuce, apples, walnuts, cheese, cranberries, sprouts, and seeds together in a large bowl or arrange on a large platter. Drizzle with dressing or serve on the side.

EnJOY!

INGREDIENTS

Maple Poppy Seed Dressing

- ¼ cup [60 ml] white wine or champagne vinegar
- ¼ cup [60 ml] chopped red onion
- ¼ cup [60 ml] pure maple syrup
- 1 teaspoon [5 ml] sea salt
- ¼ teaspoon [1.25 ml] dry ground mustard
- ½ cup [120 ml] avocado or olive oil
- 1½ teaspoons [7.5 ml] poppy seeds

Salad

- 8 cups [2 liters] mixed greens of choice
- 2 Gala, Honeycrisp, Pink Lady, or other sweet-tart apples of choice (or pears), cored and cut into thin slices
- 1 cup [240 ml] walnuts (or hickory nuts), roughly chopped
- 2 oz [56 g] sprouted alfalfa or clover (or blend of choice)
- 4 oz [113 g] Manchego or Irish cheddar cheese, thinly sliced or roughly grated
- ½ cup [120 ml] dried cranberries or tart cherries
- ¼ cup [60 ml] sprouted pumpkin seeds
- ¼ cup [60 ml] sprouted sunflower seeds
- 4 oz [113 g] chopped, cooked bacon (optional)

Makes 4 servings

EVERYWHERE IS LOCAL

BRUNCH

some nights
you just need
pancakes for dinner

Spinach Mushroom Steamed Eggs, 81

00 Florentine Egg Cups, 85

Perfectly Puffy Oven Pancake, 87

Power-Packed Pancakes, 89

Sprouted Oat-Banana Pancakes, 91

Yerba Mate Lemon Ricotta Pancakes, 93

Anney Girl's Almond Flour Cheese Blintz, 95

Adaptogenic Bircher, 97

Sprouted Oat Granola, 99

SPINACH-MUSHROOM STEAMED EGGS

In a large skillet (with well-fitting lid), sauté bacon (if using) or heat oil or butter over medium heat. If using bacon, fry until partially crisped. Add chopped red pepper and onion. Sauté for 2-3 minutes. Stir in sliced mushrooms and add 1 tablespoon [15 ml] more butter or oil. Sauté an additional 3-5 minutes.

Add chopped spinach to pan; stir until wilting begins. Sprinkle with ground black cumin. With a spoon or small spatula, create 6 nesting areas in the veggie mixture for eggs to steam, exposing bottom of pan. In each circle of exposed pan, drop 1 teaspoon [15 ml] butter or oil of choice.

Crack an egg carefully onto melted butter in circle. Sprinkle with feta cheese (or other cheese), and salt and pepper to taste. Cover pan tightly and allow to steam 3-5 minutes (3 minutes for runny yolk and 5 minutes for cooked yolk) Serve immediately.

EnJOY!

INGREDIENTS

- ¼ cup [56 g]) butter or ghee OR 4 oz [113 g] pastured bacon, chopped finely
- 2-3 tablespoons [28-42 g] additional butter, ghee, or oil of choice [30-45 ml]
- 2 oz [56 g] finely chopped red pepper
- 2 oz [56 g] finely chopped onion of choice
- 4 oz [113 g] thinly sliced mushrooms
- 8 oz [226 g] chopped fresh spinach leaves
- 6 pastured eggs
- 1 oz [28 g] crumbled feta, grated Parmesan or Asiago (optional)
- Black cumin powder
- Freshly ground black pepper
- Sea salt

Makes 3 to 6 servings

THREE BROTHERS FARM
OCONOMOWOC, WISCONSIN

When you ask a farmer if they have always wanted to be a farmer, you expect the answer to be a resounding "Yes!" When I put the question to Michael Gutschenritter of Three Brothers Farm in Oconomowoc, WI, he laughed and replied, "No."

Michael studied Spanish and creative writing at the University of Wisconsin Steven's Point. He wanted to be an editor. He also wanted his grandparent's family farm to stay in the family and be converted into a model of sustainable, organic agriculture. He admits it was an alluring, romantic idea. However, when talk of the farm being put up for sale became reality, Michael and his brother decided to take a leap into farming, despite the fact that they really didn't know what that would require of them. They held the essence of the organic farm idea while trying to decide where to begin with 100-acres, and a big financial risk in front of them.

Year one began with growing vegetables, farmer's markets, Community Supported Agriculture (CSA) subscriptions, and the assumption that this business plan would pay the mortgage. Michael soon learned the difference between his romantic ideas about farming and the very real struggle it actually is.

While persevering into year two, CSA membership doubled, the farm relinquished the laborious commitment to farmer's markets, Michael's brother decided to step out of the operation and more hands were needed to do the work. As fate would have it, Courtney, a vibrant and apprenticed farmer through the Maine Organic Farm and Garden Association, stepped in. Together, they planned, worked hard, and found that an organic farm could hold space for vegetables—and romance.

In year three, Michael and Courtney, now happily married, met Peter Sandroni, owner of Engine Company No. 3 and La Merenda restaurants. Peter wanted farm-fresh eggs at a fair price. A lot of farm-fresh eggs.

With the foresight to listen to the market, Michael and Courtney bought 600 chickens, brooded them in the basement, and began legitimate pasture-raised egg production. One thing leads to another and now, not-so-like-magic, they collect 1,100 eggs per day and pasture-raise 3,600 roasting chickens for restaurants and markets in Southeastern Wisconsin.

Their vision? Continue to listen to the market, potentially raise 6,000 roasting poultry for restaurants, grow their pastured lamb and wool production business, and use all 100 acres for sustainable soil health and animal feed. All this while cultivating Courtney's Courtney Joy Floral enterprise and welcoming a new baby to the family!

When asked how Michael and Courtney see themselves connecting to the larger world of sustainable agriculture, they recognize their opportunity to be a role-model farm for up-and-coming young farmers. They desire to generously share their knowledge through consulting and teaching, all the while bringing ethically produced food to their community. So maybe they didn't always want to be farmers; lucky for us, they are.

FLORENTINE EGG CUPS

Grease 12 large cups of a muffin tin; set aside. Preheat oven to 400 F [204 C].

In a large skillet over medium heat, sauté mushrooms and onions in fat of choice for 5-7 minutes. Add tomatoes; sauté an additional 2 minutes. Stir in spinach until wilted, about 1 minute, followed by ricotta and seasonings. Remove from heat; set aside.

Line each muffin cup with a slice of ham. Divide spinach filling between each cup, forming a pocket for the egg. Carefully crack an egg into each pocket of filling in ham cup. Sprinkle with paprika, salt and pepper to taste.

Bake 15-20 minutes (15 minutes for a soft-set yolk and up to 20 minutes for a well-set yolk.) Run a sharp knife around the edge of each ham cup. Using a large spoon, lift out onto serving dish or individual plates. Garnish as desired.

EnJOY!

Variations:

1. Vegetarian option: Increase spinach to 8 oz [226 g], replace ham or turkey with a tomato slice on bottom of muffin tin.

2. Omit ricotta and herbs de Provence and substitute with 5 oz [142 g] Boursin herbed cheese of choice.

3. Delicious with a Mornay or Hollandaise sauce.

INGREDIENTS

- 3 oz [85 g] bacon or duck lard, butter, ghee, or avocado oil
- 6 oz [170 g] mushrooms, very finely chopped
- 3 oz [85 g] onions, minced
- 3 oz [85 g] tomatoes, very finely chopped
- 6 oz [170 g] fresh spinach leaves, very finely chopped
- 5 oz [142 g] ricotta or almond milk cream cheese
- Sprinkle of garlic powder
- Sprinkle of black cumin powder
- Sea salt and pepper to taste
- ¼ teaspoon [1.25 ml] herbs de Provence
- 12 thin slices Black Forest ham or smoked turkey
- 12 pastured eggs
- Paprika
- Fresh parsley or lemon thyme for garnish (optional)

Makes 12 egg cups

EVERYWHERE IS LOCAL

PERFECTLY PUFFY OVEN PANCAKE

Heat oven to 425 F [218 C] Place a 9-inch [23 cm] round ovenproof skillet (preferably a cast-iron skillet) in the pre-heating oven.

In a medium bowl, 4-cup [1-liter] glass measure, or blender, beat eggs, flour, cream, water, and sea salt until bubbly. If you are making a savory pancake, you may add white pepper now, or vanilla for a sweet pancake.

When oven has reached 425 F [218 C], add butter to hot skillet and return to oven to melt. When butter has melted, swirl to coat bottom of pan. Carefully pour pancake batter into butter. Bake 13-15 minutes, until edges are deeply golden brown and center is just beginning to turn golden. Have your toppings ready.

Transfer to a cooling rack or trivet. Top pancake and eat immediately.

EnJOY!

Variations:

If serving as a savory dish: you may want to top with sautéed greens, bacon, ham, cheese, and/or fresh herbs.

If serving as a sweet dish: you may want to top with sifted confectioner's sugar, fresh lemon juice, drizzled chocolate, fruit preserves, pure maple syrup, and/or fresh fruit.

INGREDIENTS

- ♦ 4 tablespoons [56 g] unsalted butter, cut into pieces
- ♦ 4 pastured eggs
- ♦ 2¼ oz [64 g] GF flour blend
- ♦ ¼ cup [60 ml] cream + ¼ cup [60 ml] water

OR

- ♦ ½ cup [120 ml] whole milk or milk of choice
- ♦ ¼ teaspoon [1.25 ml] sea salt

Variations:

- ♦ 1 tablespoon [15 ml] pure vanilla (for sweet pancake)
- ♦ ⅛ teaspoon [0.6 ml] white pepper (for savory pancake)

Makes one 9-inch [23-cm] oven pancake

POWER-PACKED PANCAKES

In a large bowl, whisk together the flours, hemp seeds, flax meal, collagen powder (if using), baking powder, baking soda, sea salt, cinnamon, and cardamom. In a separate bowl or large glass measuring cup, whisk together the eggs, buttermilk, oil or butter, and vanilla. (If using milk + lemon juice, allow milk to sit 5-7 minutes before combining with eggs.)

Pour the wet ingredients into the dry ingredients, stirring to combine. Stir until the mixture is fairly smooth. Allow the batter to rest, uncovered, for 10 minutes.

While the batter is resting, heat a large skillet over medium heat or preheat a griddle to 350 F [176 C], until the surface is hot enough for a droplet of water to skitter across it. Lightly grease the pan with butter or oil.

Pour the batter, ¼ cup [60 ml] at a time, onto the hot surface. Cook pancakes on the first side until bubbles form on the tops and the bottoms are brown, about 1-2 minutes. Flip and cook until the bottoms are brown, 1-2 minutes longer. Serve immediately, or hold briefly in a warm oven.

For grain-free pancakes: Omit GF flour blend, increase almond flour by 4 oz [113 g] (6 oz [170 g] total almond flour) and add 1 oz [28 g] arrowroot powder.

EnJOY!

Variations:

Add in ½ cup [120 ml] chopped nuts, mini-chocolate chips, blueberries, raspberries, diced banana, sliced strawberries, or unsweetened shredded coconut

This recipe is wonderful for waffles!

INGREDIENTS

- ♦ 4 oz [113g] GF flour blend
- ♦ 2 oz [56 g] almond flour or GF flour blend
- ♦ ½ oz [14 g] coconut flour
- ♦ ½ oz [14 g] hemp seeds
- ♦ ½ oz [14 g] flax meal
- ♦ ¼ oz [7 g] multi-collagen powder (optional)
- ♦ 2 teaspoons [10 ml] baking powder
- ♦ 1 teaspoon [5 ml] baking soda
- ♦ ¼ teaspoon [1.25 ml] sea salt
- ♦ ¼ teaspoon [1.25 ml] Ceylon cinnamon
- ♦ Pinch cardamom
- ♦ 2 pastured eggs
- ♦ 1½ cups [360 ml] buttermilk, pourable yogurt, (or other milk of choice + 1 tablespoon [15 ml] fresh lemon juice or apple cider vinegar)
- ♦ 2 tablespoons [30 ml] avocado oil, melted butter or ghee, or coconut oil
- ♦ 1 tablespoon [15 ml] pure vanilla or spiced rum
- ♦ Butter, avocado oil, or coconut oil for greasing skillet

Makes 10 4-inch [10-cm] pancakes

SPROUTED-OAT BANANA PANCAKES

COMPOTE

Place blueberries, water, lemon zest, cinnamon and ginger in a medium-size saucepan. Bring to a boil, reduce heat and simmer over medium-low heat, stirring occasionally, 20 minutes. In a small bowl, stir arrowroot powder into 2 tablespoons [30 ml] water until dissolved. Stir dissolved arrowroot and vanilla extract into blueberry mixture and heat one minute more, or until thickened.

PANCAKES

Combine oats, baking powder, sea salt, yogurt, and banana in a blender pitcher. Blend until smooth, stopping the blender and stirring the mixture with a spatula as necessary to keep it moving. Add eggs, pure maple syrup, vanilla, and melted butter or oil, and blend just until combined. (If your batter seems too thick, add milk to the blender a little at a time until it reaches your desired consistency.)

Heat a large skillet over medium heat until hot; add 2-3 teaspoons [10-15 g] butter and swirl to coat. Pour batter by ¼-cupfuls [60-ml] onto hot skillet and cook until batter starts to bubble and dry around edges. (If batter seems to be cooking too fast, reduce heat; too slow, increase heat slightly.) Flip and cook through. Transfer to serving plate and repeat with remaining batter.

Serve pancakes with yogurt and blueberry compote as desired.

EnJOY!

INGREDIENTS

Blueberry Compote (optional for serving)

♦ 7 oz [200 g] fresh or frozen blueberries
♦ ½ cup [120 ml] water
♦ Zest of 1 lemon
♦ 1 teaspoon [5 ml] ground Ceylon cinnamon
♦ 1 tablespoon [15 ml] fresh grated ginger or ¼ teaspoon [1.25 ml] ground ginger
♦ 2 teaspoons [10 ml] arrowroot powder or cornstarch
♦ 1 teaspoon [5 ml] pure vanilla

Pancakes

♦ 6 oz [170 g] sprouted rolled oats
♦ 2 teaspoons [20 ml] baking powder
♦ ¼ teaspoon [1.25 ml] sea salt
♦ 1 cup [240 ml] plain yogurt, cream, or milk of choice
♦ 1 ripe banana, cut into chunks
♦ 2 pastured eggs, room temperature
♦ 2 tablespoons [30 ml] pure maple syrup
♦ 2 teaspoons [10 ml] pure vanilla or spiced rum
♦ 2 tablespoons [30 ml] avocado oil or melted butter or ghee
♦ Butter, avocado oil, or coconut oil for greasing skillet
♦ Yogurt (optional for serving)

Serves 4

YERBA MATE LEMON RICOTTA PANCAKES

Place the egg whites in the bowl of a stand mixer or with an electric mixer in a glass bowl, beat for 5 minutes on medium-high speed until soft peaks form. Meanwhile, whisk together flours, yerba mate, maca (if using), baking powder, sugar, and sea salt in a medium mixing bowl. In another bowl, whisk together the egg yolks, ricotta, cream, lemon juice, and lemon zest.

On slow speed, beat dry ingredients into yolk-ricotta mixture. Fold in the whipped egg whites until combined.

Heat a large skillet or griddle over medium heat (or 350 F [176 C]). Melt up to 1 tablespoon [15 ml] butter, ghee, or oil in the pan or griddle, brushing to coat.

Using a 2-inch [5 cm] batter scoop, scoop pancake mixture into the pan, gently spreading batter into 3-inch [8 cm] circle. Fry until bottoms are golden brown and edges begin to dry. Using a spatula, flip each pancake and cook until second side is golden brown and center is cooked through. Adjust temperature as necessary. Serve with lemon wedges, butter, and maple syrup.

EnJOY!

INGREDIENTS

- 4 pastured eggs, separated
- 4 oz [113 g] almond flour or 5½ oz [156 g] GF flour blend
- ½ oz [14 g] coconut flour
- 1-2 tablespoons [15-30 ml] ground and sifted dry yerba mate tea
- ½ teaspoon [2.5 ml] maca powder (optional)
- 2 teaspoons [10 ml] baking powder
- 1 tablespoon [15 ml] coconut sugar, maple sugar or unrefined cane sugar
- ½ teaspoon [2.5 ml] sea salt
- 1 cup [240 ml] whole milk ricotta cheese or dairy-free cream cheese
- 1 cup [240 ml] cream or full-fat coconut milk
- 2 tablespoons [30 ml] fresh lemon juice
- 1 tablespoon [15 ml] finely chopped fresh lemon zest
- Butter, ghee, avocado or coconut oil for frying
- Lemon wedges, butter and maple syrup, for serving

Makes 14-16 3-inch [8-cm] pancakes

ANNEY GIRL'S ALMOND FLOUR CHEESE BLINTZ

Anne fell in love with cheese blintzes when we were on vacation at Marco Island, Florida. She was ten, and although more than a decade has passed, it's still a special treat when we enjoy a family breakfast of blintzes and wonderful memories. Now it's time to make some memories of your own.

CREPES

Stir gelatin into ½ cup [120 ml] water in a small bowl; set aside for 3 minutes to bloom.

Meanwhile combine almond flour, sea salt, eggs, melted butter, buttermilk, and vanilla in a blender. Blend until smooth. Add gelatin mixture to the blender and blend until smooth.

Heat an 8-inch [20-cm] oiled frying pan over medium heat. When hot, pour ¼ cup [60 ml] batter into the pan and quickly tilt in a circle repeatedly, to spread batter evenly into a thin layer. Cook for about 2 minutes until the edges are dry and the bottom begins to turn golden, then carefully flip and cook for another minute on the other side. Set each crepe between parchment or waxed paper on a plate until ready to fill.

RICOTTA FILLING

In a medium mixing bowl, beat the cream cheese until fluffy. Add the beaten egg a little at a time, beating until smooth after each addition; scrape the sides of the bowl. Add the lemon zest, lemon juice, vanilla, sea salt, and sugar, and mix until well combined. Fold in the ricotta cheese.

TO ASSEMBLE

Place approximately 3 tablespoons [45 ml] filling about 2 inches [5 cm] from the top of each crepe. Fold the sides in, fold the top down, then loosely roll the crepe into a log. Heat 2 tablespoons butter [28 g] or oil [30 ml] in a large frying pan until sizzling. Sauté the blintzes until lightly browned and heated through. Top with fresh fruit, warmed fruit compote, or preserves.

EnJOY!

INGREDIENTS

Crepes

- 2 tablespoons [30 ml] grass-fed gelatin powder
- ½ cup [120 ml] water
- 3¾ oz [106 g] almond flour
- ¼ teaspoon [1.25 ml] sea salt
- 4 pastured eggs
- ½ cup [120 ml] buttermilk, coconut kefir, plain yogurt, or water
- 2 tablespoons [30 ml] melted butter, ghee, or coconut oil
- 1 teaspoon [5 ml] pure vanilla

Ricotta Filling

- 3 oz [85 g] cream cheese, at room temperature
- 1 pastured egg, lightly beaten
- 2 teaspoons [10 ml] lemon zest
- 1 teaspoon [5 ml] fresh lemon juice
- 2 teaspoons [10 ml] pure vanilla
- ¼ teaspoon [1.25 ml] sea salt
- 1 oz [28 g] refined or unrefined cane sugar
- 12 oz [340 g] ricotta cheese

Makes 8 to 10 blintzes

ADAPTOGENIC BIRCHER

Combine all ingredients in a large bowl and mix thoroughly. Transfer bircher to a wide-mouth quart [1 liter] jar. Cover and place in refrigerator overnight. Store covered in the fridge for up to 3 days.

EnJOY!

Topping ideas:

♦ Fresh berries
♦ Pure maple syrup
♦ Honey
♦ Banana
♦ Nuts
♦ Seeds
♦ Sprouted granola

INGREDIENTS

♦ 1½ cups [120 g] sprouted rolled oats
♦ 1 apple, finely chopped or grated
♦ 1 cup [240 ml] full fat coconut milk, almond milk
OR ½ cup [120 ml] cream + ½ cup [120 ml] water
♦ 1 cup [240 ml] plain or vanilla yogurt of choice
♦ ¼ cup [60 ml] tart dried cherries, cranberries, or raisins
♦ ¼ cup [60 ml] chopped sprouted sea salted almonds
♦ 2-3 tablespoons [30-45 ml] raw local honey
♦ 2 tablespoons [30 ml] fresh lemon juice
♦ 2 tablespoons [30 ml] MCT oil
♦ 1 tablespoon [15 ml] multi-collagen powder (optional)
♦ 1 tablespoon [15 ml] ground coconut/flax/chia blend
♦ ½ teaspoon [2.5 ml] Ceylon cinnamon
♦ ½ teaspoon [2.5 ml] maca root powder
♦ ½ teaspoon [2.5 ml] ashwagandha powder
♦ ¼ teaspoon [1.25 ml] American ginseng powder
♦ Pinch nutmeg
♦ Pinch cardamom

Makes 1 quart [1 liter]

EVERYWHERE IS LOCAL

SPROUTED OAT AND NUT GRANOLA

Preheat the oven to 300 F [148 C] and line a large, rimmed baking sheet with parchment paper; set aside.

In a large bowl, mix together the oats, flax seed meal, chia seeds, shredded coconut, pumpkin seeds, nuts, apricot kernels (if using), cinnamon, and sea salt.

In a small saucepan, bring water and coconut oil just to simmer (tiny air bubbles form). Meanwhile, in a 2-cup [480-ml] glass measure, stir together honey, maple syrup, vanilla, and almond extract. Pour coconut-oil water into honey mixture and whisk until combined.

Pour the wet ingredients over the dry ingredients and stir until evenly coated. Spread the mixture onto prepared baking sheet, and press it into an even, compact layer. Bake 30 minutes, then stir gently. Bake 10 minutes; stir again. Bake another 10 minutes, until granola is toasted and golden. Cool completely, then stir in dried fruit. Store in an airtight container at room temperature for up to 3 weeks.

EnJOY!

INGREDIENTS

- 18 oz [510 g] sprouted old-fashioned rolled oats
- 2 oz [56 g] golden flax seed meal
- 1 oz [28 g] chia seeds
- 4 oz [113 g] unsweetened shredded coconut
- 3 oz [84 g] sprouted pumpkin seeds
- 4 oz [113 g] sprouted almonds, walnuts, or pecans, chopped
- 2 oz [56 g] sweet apricot kernels, chopped (optional)
- 1 teaspoon [5 ml] Ceylon cinnamon
- 1½ teaspoons [7.5 ml] sea salt
- ½ cup [120 ml] unrefined coconut oil
- ½ cup [120 ml] boiling water
- ½ cup [120 ml] raw, local honey
- ¼ cup [60 ml] pure maple syrup
- 1 teaspoon [5 ml] pure vanilla extract
- ¼ teaspoon [1.25 ml] pure almond extract
- 6 oz [168 g] dried tart cherries (or raisins)
- 3 oz [84 g] finely chopped dried apricot (or other dried fruit of choice)

Makes about 2 quarts [2 liters]

MAINS

maybe it's Taco Tuesday
or Pizza Friday
maybe it's leftovers
all week long
dining solo in self-care
or community table creation
delight in every bite

Maria's Swedish Salmon, 105

Shepherd's Pie, 107

Chicken Florentine Casserole,111

Turkey-Broccoli-Wild Rice Casserole, 113

Creamy Mushroom Green Bean Bake, 115

Marvelous Meatloaf, 117

Garlic Butter Steak & Snow Pea Stirfry, 119

Fajita-Seasoned Fish Tacos, 121

Cauliflower Tikka Masala, 123

MARIA'S SWEDISH SALMON

Preheat the oven to 400 F [204 C]

Chop the Savoy cabbage into 8 equal wedge portions; set aside.

Line a rimmed baking sheet or other large baking dish with parchment paper (or grease with avocado oil or butter). Place cabbage and salmon pieces onto prepared baking sheet. Sprinkle chopped leeks and chili pepper slices over all.

In a small bowl or glass measure, combine the avocado oil, tamari sauce, and lime zest. Pour over cabbage and salmon on baking sheet.

Place the baking sheet on the center rack in oven; bake for 18-20 minutes (until cabbage is fork-tender). Then broil for 5 minutes until salmon is done and cabbage is crisp on the outside.

While the salmon and cabbage are baking, mix the mayonnaise, lime juice, water, and sea salt in a small bowl or glass measure. Drizzle mayonnaise sauce over baked salmon and cabbage, then sprinkle with sesame seeds and nuts (optional).

EnJOY!

INGREDIENTS

- ½ Savoy cabbage (or 4 cups Brussels sprouts, trimmed and halved)
- 4-4 oz [113 g] pieces wild-caught salmon
- 1 leek, rinsed, white and tender green parts chopped into ½-inch [1-cm] pieces
- 1 small hot red chili pepper (serrano), seeded and very finely sliced
- 4 tablespoons [60 ml] avocado or olive oil
- 4 tablespoons [60 ml] tamari sauce
- 2 teaspoons [10 ml] lime zest
- ½ cup [120 ml] mayonnaise
- Juice of 1 lime
- 2 tablespoons [30 ml] water
- ½ teaspoon [2.5 ml] sea salt
- 2 tablespoons [30 ml] black sesame seeds
- 4 oz [113 g] pistachios or almonds, coarsely chopped (optional)

Makes 4 servings

SHEPHERD'S PIE

Preheat oven to 375 F [190 C]. Bring 1 quart [1 liter] water to boil, add potatoes and simmer partially covered on med-low 17-20 minutes until potatoes are fork tender. Drain water from potatoes, keeping potatoes in pot. Add butter, cream, parsley, sea salt, and pepper. Mash with hand-held potato masher. Cover and set aside.

While potatoes are boiling, in a large cast iron skillet, over medium-high heat, heat the avocado oil. Add onion, carrot, garlic, and lamb. Cook until browned, 8-10 minutes.

Sprinkle rice flour over meat mixture. Cook additional 1 minute. Slowly pour in bone broth, stirring well. Add Worcestershire sauce, tomato paste (if using), red wine or apple cider vinegar, herbs, salt, and pepper. Simmer until the juices thicken, about 10 minutes, then add the pea shoots and/or peas.

Spoon mashed potatoes over meat mixture in skillet. Sprinkle with Cheddar cheese. Bake until golden, 30-35 minutes.

EnJOY!

Makes 4 servings

INGREDIENTS

- 1½ lbs [680 g] potatoes (your choice), peeled and cut into 1-inch cubes
- 4 tablespoons [57 g] butter, room temperature
- ¼ cup [60 ml] heavy cream or non-dairy alternative of choice
- 1 tablespoon [15 ml] fresh parsley, finely chopped
- ¼ teaspoon [1.25 ml] sea salt
- ⅛ teaspoon [.6 ml] black pepper
- 2 tablespoons [30 ml] avocado oil or butter
- 1 lb [454 g] ground pastured lamb
- ½ cup [120 ml] diced shallot or yellow onion
- 1 cup [240 ml] diced carrot
- 2-3 cloves garlic minced
- 1 tablespoon [15 ml] white rice flour
- 1 cup [240 ml] beef bone broth
- 1 teaspoon [5 ml] Worcestershire sauce
- 1 tablespoon [15 ml] tomato paste (optional)
- ¼ cup [60 ml] red wine (optional) or 2 T [30 ml] apple cider vinegar
- 2 teaspoons [10 ml] fresh rosemary leaves, minced
- 1 teaspoon [5 ml] fresh thyme leaves
- 1 teaspoon [5 ml] sea salt
- ¼ teaspoon [1.25 ml] freshly ground black pepper
- 1 oz [28 g] finely chopped fresh pea shoots (or 1 cup [240 ml] frozen peas, or both peas and shoots)
- 4 oz [113 g] Irish Cheddar cheese (like Dubliner), shredded

BELFRĒ KITCHEN, DELAFIELD, WISCONSIN

Not all restaurateurs come from generations of restauranteurs. Some simply come from a passion to bring the best sustainably grown, local ingredients to a food-truck enterprise. Until the food-truck thing doesn't happen because you find a historic church in a quaint downtown to transform into a favorite culinary hotspot for the community you live in.

Meet Amy Quinn: former special-needs educator turned farm-to-table restaurant owner of Belfrē Kitchen in Delafield, Wisconsin. Amy grew up in California surrounded by a rich array of agriculture—even at home.

Breakfasts involved backyard berry-picking to top cereal, and begging Mom for "real orange juice" (like her friends had from the frozen cardboard tube) rather than fresh-squeezed from the massive tree outside her window. Amy walked by apricot and nut orchards on her way to school and dreamed of being a farmer one day.

So the growing up to be a farmer one day didn't happen, but the farmer-inside is obvious as Amy's inspiration has unfolded thus far. This inspiration sometimes bumps into realism when opening a farm-to-table restaurant. Amy learned early on that obtaining quality ingredients within razor-thin margins is hard enough work anyway, but sourcing large quantities of local, organic ingredients for a reasonably-priced menu and profitable business can be daunting.

What's undaunted is the commitment for communicating Belfrē Kitchen's support of sustainable agriculture. To do this, she works with Joe Kolafa, general manager extraordinaire. Together, they bring in fabulous products from local farmers and let their clients know, not only through name-dropping on the menu, but through "Meet Your Farmer" dinners as well.

Amy, Joe, Chef Jason and the culinary staff take their inspiration from seasonal produce and mindfully-raised meat to create intentionally-crafted menu items that delight their guests.

And speaking of guests, the joy-spark of Amy's dedication is found in expanded community collaboration between her guests and local artists, musicians, special celebrations and towny happenings- all while providing a delicious dining experience.

This is what happens when food-truck vision becomes farm-to-table fabulous!

CHICKEN FLORENTINE CASSEROLE

Preheat oven to 375 F [190 C]. Grease a 7x11-inch [18x28-cm] or 2-qt [2-liter] baking dish; set aside.

Melt 6 tablespoons [85 g] butter over medium heat in large sauté pan. Add sliced mushrooms and rosemary; sauté 5 minutes. Stir in minced garlic and sea salt; sauté an additional 2 minutes.

Stir fresh spinach leaves into mushroom mixture in sauté pan. Cover pan to steam and wilt spinach; about 1-2 minutes. When spinach is wilted, stir in cooked chicken, Manchego and Boursin cheese. Transfer all to prepared baking dish.

Sprinkle with paprika. Bake for 25 minutes until bubbly.

EnJOY!

INGREDIENTS

♦ 6 tablespoons [85 g] butter

♦ 8 oz [227 g] mushrooms, sliced

♦ 1 teaspoon [5 ml] minced fresh rosemary leaves

♦ 3 cloves garlic, minced

♦ ½ teaspoon [5 ml] sea salt

♦ 1.25 lbs [567 g] cooked chicken or turkey, chopped

♦ 8 oz [227 g] fresh spinach leaves, chopped

♦ 1 cup [240 ml] heavy cream or milk of choice

♦ 2 cups [480 ml] shredded Manchego cheese

♦ 5 oz [142 g] Boursin Shallot & Chive cheese (5 oz mascarpone or cream cheese + ¼ tsp onion powder may be substituted for the Boursin)

♦ Paprika

Makes 4 servings

EVERYWHERE IS LOCAL

TURKEY-BROCCOLI-WILD RICE CASSEROLE

Butter a 6-qt [6-liter] enamel cast iron Dutch oven (or 9x13-inch [23x33 cm]); set aside. Preheat oven to 375 F [190 C].

Cook the wild rice or sprouted brown rice or quinoa according to package instructions. While rice is cooking, heat a large skillet over medium heat. When hot, add avocado oil and butter. Stir in diced onions; sauté 5 minutes. Add sliced mushrooms, stir, and sauté 5 minutes. Stir in minced garlic and cook an additional 2 minutes. Add cooked turkey or chicken and sprinkle with salt and pepper to taste.

While onions and mushrooms are cooking, steam broccoli for 7 minutes; set aside.

In a large mixing bowl or 8-cup [2-liter] measure, combine cream of chicken soup, cream of mushroom soup, sour cream, cream, lemon juice, herbs de Provence, paprika, and shredded Swiss cheese.

Layer the cooked wild rice (brown rice, quinoa), steamed broccoli, and turkey or chicken mixture in the prepared Dutch oven. Pour soup mixture over all. Sprinkle shredded cheddar over top. Bake 35-45 minutes, until cheese is melted and bubbly.

EnJOY!

INGREDIENTS

- 6 oz [170 g] wild rice or sprouted brown rice or quinoa
- 12 oz [340 g] fresh broccoli florets and stems, coarsely chopped
- 2 tablespoons [30 ml] avocado or olive oil
- 3 tablespoons [42 g] butter
- 4 oz [113 g] diced yellow onion
- 8 oz [227 g] mushrooms of choice, thinly sliced
- 2 cloves garlic, minced
- 1 lb [454 g] cooked turkey or chicken, chopped coarsely
- Sea salt and pepper to taste
- 2 12-oz [340 g] containers organic condensed cream of chicken soup
- 1 12-oz [340 g] container organic cream of mushroom soup
- 1 cup [240 ml] sour cream or plain Greek yogurt
- 1 cup [240 ml] heavy cream or milk of choice
- ¼ cup [60 ml] fresh lemon juice
- ½ teaspoon [2.5 ml] herbs de Provence
- 1 teaspoon [5 ml] sweet paprika
- 2 teaspoons fresh minced rosemary
- 8 oz [227 g] shredded Swiss cheese
- 4 oz [113 g] shredded sharp Cheddar cheese

Makes 6 servings

CREAMY MUSHROOM-GREEN BEAN BAKE

Preheat oven to 450 F [232 C]. Grease a 2-quart [2-liter] casserole; set aside.

BEAN PREPATION

Bring a gallon [4 liters] of water and 2 tablespoons [30 ml] of sea salt to a boil in an 8-quart [8-liter] saucepan. Add the beans and blanch for 5 minutes. Drain in a colander and immediately plunge the beans into a large bowl of ice water to stop the cooking. Drain and place in prepared casserole; set aside.

MUSHROOM SAUCE

Melt butter in a 12-inch [30-cm] cast iron skillet set over medium heat. Add the onions and allow to cook, undisturbed, for 5-7 minutes. Stir in mushrooms, sea salt, and pepper and cook, stirring occasionally, until the mushrooms begin to give up some of their liquid, approximately 4-5 minutes. Add the garlic and thyme leaves, and continue to cook for another 1-2 minutes. Sprinkle the flour over the mixture and stir to combine. Cook for 1 minute. Add the broth and simmer for 1 minute. Decrease the heat to medium-low and add the cream. Cook until the mixture thickens, stirring occasionally, approximately 6-8 minutes.

Stir in lemon juice or white wine and nutmeg. Salt and pepper to taste.

Pour the mushroom sauce over the green beans in the casserole. Top with fried onions. Bake until bubbly, approximately 15 minutes. Remove and serve immediately.

EnJOY!

Variation:

Add ½ lb [226 g] cooked ground beef to the mushroom sauce.

INGREDIENTS

♦ 1 lb [454 g] fresh green beans, rinsed and trimmed
♦ 3-4 oz [85-113 g] GF French-fried onions

Mushroom Sauce

♦ 4 tablespoons [56 g] unsalted butter, ghee or avocado oil
♦ 1 large yellow onion, diced
♦ 1 lb [454 g] baby portobello mushrooms, halved and sliced
♦ 1 teaspoon [5 ml] sea salt
♦ ¼ teaspoon [1.25 ml] fresh ground black pepper
♦ 2 cloves garlic, minced
♦ 2 sprigs fresh thyme, de-stemmed
♦ 2 tablespoons [30 ml] GF flour blend
♦ 1 cup [240 ml] chicken bone broth or vegetable broth
♦ 1 cup [240 ml] cream or full fat coconut milk
♦ 1 tablespoon [15 ml] fresh lemon juice or white wine
♦ ¼ teaspoon [1.25 ml] nutmeg
♦ Sea salt & pepper to taste

Makes 4 to 6 servings

MARVELOUS MEATLOAF

Preheat oven to 350 F [176 C]. In a large mixing bowl, combine all ingredients by hand or use a stand mixer.

Pat meat mixture into loaf-shape in an 8x4-inch [20x10 cm] loaf pan. Pour additional BBQ sauce or ketchup over top as desired. Bake 1 hour. Remove from oven and allow to rest 5 minutes before slicing.

EnJOY!

INGREDIENTS

♦ 1½ lbs [680 g] ground pastured pork

♦ 1½ lbs [680 g] ground pastured beef

♦ 3 cups [720 ml] fresh breadcrumbs of choice (to make, pulse fresh bread pieces in a food processor)

♦ 1 cup [240 ml] finely diced yellow onion

♦ 1 cup [240 ml] milk of choice

♦ ¼ cup [60 ml] chopped fresh parsley

♦ 2 pastured eggs

♦ 2 garlic cloves, minced

♦ 2 tablespoons [30 ml] hemp seeds

♦ 2 tablespoons [30 ml] BBQ sauce (I use Triple Crown Organic Original BBQ Sauce brand)

♦ 1 tablespoon [15 ml] Worcestershire sauce

♦ 2 teaspoons [10 ml] sea salt

♦ ½ teaspoon [2.5 ml] freshly ground black pepper

♦ ½ teaspoon [2.5 ml] dry sage

♦ ½ teaspoon [2.5 ml] dry mustard powder

Makes one 8x4-inch [20x10 cm] loaf

GARLIC-BUTTER STEAK & SNOW PEA STIR-FRY

In a medium-sized bowl or large glass pie dish, mix together tamari sauce, cornstarch, and fresh ginger. Add sliced steak and toss until all meat is coated with the marinade; set aside.

Bring a large, deep cast iron skillet or wok to high heat and add oil. When oil just begins to smoke, add marinated steak in small batches (to avoid crowding). Cook the meat until slightly crispy (about 2-3 minutes per batch), stirring frequently; remove to platter. When all steak is cooked, turn heat to medium.

Add butter, bone broth, and garlic to skillet, bringing sauce to a simmer. Allow to cook for 2-3 minutes until garlic is fragrant. Add in shiitake mushrooms and cook for 2 minutes. Add snow peas, cover and cook an additional 2 minutes. Return steak to pan and toss everything together. Sprinkle with green onions (optional). Serve warm as is or over steamed sprouted brown rice.

EnJOY!

INGREDIENTS

♦ 2 lbs [900 g] skirt, flank, or flat iron steak, slightly frozen then cut into ⅛-inch [3 mm] strips

♦ ¼ cup [60 ml] tamari sauce or coconut aminos

♦ 2 tablespoons [30 ml] cornstarch

♦ 2 teaspoons [20 ml] minced fresh ginger root

♦ 1 tablespoon [15 ml] avocado or peanut oil

♦ 4 tablespoons [56 g] butter

♦ ¼ cup [60 ml] beef or chicken bone broth

♦ 4 garlic cloves, minced

♦ 1 lb [454 g] snow peas, trimmed

♦ 4 oz [113 g] shitake mushrooms, cut into thin strips

♦ Green onions, sliced diagonally for garnish (optional)

Makes 4 to 6 servings

FAJITA-SEASONED FISH TACOS

Preheat oven to 400 F [204 C]. Combine all fish taco sauce ingredients in a small bowl; set aside. Combine fajita seasoning ingredients and rub into fish pieces. Place fish on a parchment-lined pan and drizzle with avocado oil. Bake for 12-15 minutes or until flaky and cooked through. Heat tortillas according to package directions. Divide fish between tortillas. Top as desired and serve.

EnJOY!

INGREDIENTS

♦ 1½ lb [680 g] wild Alaskan black bass or wild cod, cut into small chunks

♦ Avocado or olive oil

♦ 8 6-inch [15 cm] grain-free or sprouted corn tortillas

♦ 1 sliced avocado

♦ 1 lime, cut into wedges

♦ Shredded Cheddar or Monterey Jack cheese or queso blanco

♦ Fresh diced tomatoes or salsa

♦ Fresh cilantro

Fajita Seasoning

♦ 2 teaspoons [10 ml] chili powder

♦ 1 teaspoon [5 ml] sea salt

♦ 1 teaspoon [5 ml] paprika

♦ 1 teaspoon [5 ml] brown sugar or coconut sugar

♦ ½ teaspoon [2.5 ml] ground black pepper

♦ ½ teaspoon [2.5 ml] onion powder

♦ ½ teaspoon [2.5 ml] garlic powder

♦ ½ teaspoon [2.5 ml] oregano

♦ ½ teaspoon [2.5 ml] ground cumin

♦ ¼ teaspoon [1.25 ml] cayenne pepper

Fish Taco Sauce

♦ 2 tablespoons [30 ml] mayonnaise

♦ 3 tablespoons [45 ml] sour cream or plain yogurt

♦ ½ lime, juiced

♦ ½ teaspoon [2.5 ml] garlic powder

♦ ½ teaspoon [2.5 ml] ground cumin

♦ ¼ teaspoon [1.25 ml] sriracha

Makes 4 to 6 servings

CAULIFLOWER TIKKA MASALA

Preheat oven to 400 F [204 C]. Line a baking sheet with parchment paper, set aside.

VEGETABLES

Slice the cauliflower florets off the head of cauliflower. Chop the remaining stalk into bite-sized pieces. Place cauliflower, carrots, and potatoes in a large mixing bowl. In a small bowl, combine garam masala, coriander, turmeric, and sea salt. Drizzle oil over cauliflower, carrots, and potatoes and season with the spice mix; toss to coat. Pour vegetables onto the prepared baking sheet and roast for 25-30 minutes until vegetables are fork-tender .

TIKKA MASALA CURRY SAUCE

While vegetables are roasting, sauté the onion in butter or oil until soft and translucent, 5-7 minutes, over medium heat. While onions are sautéing, add garam masala, paprika, coriander, cumin, turmeric, chili powder, and cardamom to the pan. At the end of 5-7 minutes, add frozen peas, garlic, and ginger; sauté for 2 minutes more. Stir in the tomatoes and tomato paste; simmer for 5 minutes. Add the coconut milk or cream and sugar; simmer for 5 minutes more. Stir in the roasted vegetables and simmer for 5-10 minutes. Add an additional 2 tablespoons [28 g] butter if desired. Delicious with naan bread!

EnJOY!

Makes 4 servings

INGREDIENTS

Vegetables

- 24 oz [680 g] cauliflower
- 12 oz [340 g] carrots, scrubbed and chopped
- 20 oz [567 g] potatoes, peeled and chopped
- 4 tablespoons [60 ml] avocado or melted coconut oil
- 1 teaspoon [5 ml] garam masala
- 2 teaspoons [10 ml] ground coriander
- ¼ teaspoon [1.25 ml] ground turmeric
- 2 teaspoons [10 ml] sea salt

Tikka Masala Curry Sauce

- 1 onion finely chopped
- 4 tablespoons [56 g] butter or ghee, or avocado oil [60ml]
- 1 cup [240 ml] frozen peas
- 3-4 garlic cloves, minced
- 2 teaspoons [10 ml] fresh ginger, minced finely or grated
- 2 teaspoons [10 ml] garam masala
- 2 teaspoons [10 ml] paprika
- 2 teaspoons [10 ml] ground coriander
- 1 teaspoon [5 ml] ground cumin
- 1 teaspoon [5 ml] ground turmeric
- ½ teaspoon [2.5 ml] ground cardamom
- 2-14oz [400 g] jars crushed tomatoes
- 2 tablespoons [30 ml] tomato paste
- 1 cup [240 ml] full-fat coconut milk or heavy whipping cream
- 1-2 teaspoons [5-10 ml] unrefined sugar or honey
- 2 tablespoons [28 g] butter or ghee (optional)
- Sea salt and pepper to taste

EVERYWHERE IS LOCAL

BREADS, QUICKBREADS, & MUFFINS

breadmaking is the art of a patient food scientist

Summer Squash Spice Bread, 129

Coconut Flour Banana Chocolate Chip Muffins, 131

Tigernut Orange-Cherry Scones, 133

Miss Mary's Cinnamon Rolls, 135

Coconut Flour Sprouted Corn Bread, 139

Sweet Potato Sprouted Oat Rolls, 141

Sprouted Brown Rice Flour Pizza Crust, 143

Sprouted Brown Rice Flour Naan, 145

Sprouted Chickpea Flour Flatbread, 147

BREADS, QUICKBREADS & MUFFINS   127

SUMMER SQUASH SPICE BREAD

Lightly grease three 2.5x5-inch [6x12-cm] loaf pans and line with parchment paper to overhang sides for easy bread removal. Preheat oven to 350F [176C].

In a medium mixing bowl, combine the flour, sugar, baking powder, baking soda, sea salt, cinnamon, ginger, nutmeg, and cardamom. Whisk together; set aside.

In a separate medium bowl or 4-cup [1-liter] glass measure, beat the oil, eggs, yogurt, and lemon zest together with a hand mixer or wire whip.

Combine the wet and dry ingredients in one bowl. Add the grated summer squash. Using a rubber spatula, stir all just until combined.

Divide the batter between the three loaf pans (about 12 oz [340 g] in each). You can use a food scale for this.

Bake until golden brown and a toothpick inserted into center comes out with crumbs only, no wet batter, about 35 to 36 minutes. Cool in pan on cooling rack for 10 to 15 minutes. Remove from pan and let cool completely on wire rack before slicing.

EnJOY!

INGREDIENTS

- 6 tablespoons [90 ml] avocado oil (or melted butter or coconut oil)
- 2 pastured eggs
- ½ cup [120 ml] plain yogurt or kefir
- 1 teaspoon [5 ml] pure vanilla
- 2 teaspoons [10 ml] finely chopped fresh lemon zest
- 10½ oz [298 g] GF flour blend (or 5 oz [142 g] almond flour + 5½ oz [156 g] GF flour blend)
- 5 oz [142 g] unrefined cane sugar (or coconut sugar, brown sugar or monk fruit)
- 1 teaspoon [5 ml] baking powder
- 1 teaspoon [5 ml] baking soda
- 1 teaspoon [5 ml] sea salt
- 2 teaspoon [10 ml] Ceylon cinnamon
- 1 teaspoon [5 ml] ground ginger
- ¼ teaspoon [1.25 ml] cardamom
- ¼ teaspoon [1.25 ml] nutmeg
- 5 oz [142 g] summer squash (yellow squash or zucchini or both), grated

Makes 3 small loaves

EVERYWHERE IS LOCAL

COCONUT FLOUR BANANA CHOCOLATE CHIP MUFFINS

Preheat oven to 350 F [176 C]. Line 12-muffin-cup tin with paper liners; set aside.

In a medium bowl, combine coconut flour, coconut sugar, arrowroot powder, and baking soda; set aside. In a separate medium bowl or glass measure, whisk together melted coconut oil, eggs, mashed banana, and vanilla.

Add dry ingredients to egg mixture; stirring until combined. Stir in chocolate chips. Scoop out evenly between muffin cups. Bake 20-22 minutes. Immediately remove muffins from tin to cooling rack.

EnJOY!

Variations:

- Add ½ cup [120 ml] chopped nuts of choice to the muffin batter.
- Substitute ¾ cup [180 ml] cooked and mashed sweet potato or pumpkin plus ¼ cup [60 ml] water for the banana.
- Omit banana and chocolate chips and add 1 cup [240 ml] finely chopped or grated apple and 1 teaspoon [5 ml] pumpkin pie spice blend to the batter.
- Sprinkle shredded unsweetened coconut on muffins before baking.
- Sprinkle finely chopped nuts on muffins before baking.

INGREDIENTS

- 2 oz [56 g] coconut flour
- 3 oz [85 g] coconut sugar or unrefined cane sugar
- 1 oz [28 g] arrowroot or tapioca powder
- 1 teaspoon [5 ml] baking soda
- ⅓ cup [80 ml] melted coconut oil, ghee, or butter
- 4 pastured eggs, room temperature
- 1 cup [240 ml] mashed banana (approximately 3 bananas)
- 2 teaspoons [10 ml] pure vanilla
- 2 oz [56 g] mini chocolate chips (or regular chocolate chips or chocolate chunks of choice)

Makes 12 muffins

TIGERNUT-ORANGE-CHERRY SCONES

Preheat oven to 400 F [204 C]. Line a large baking sheet with parchment paper; set aside.

In the bowl of a stand mixer, whisk together flours, sugar, orange zest, baking powder, and sea salt. Add cold, diced butter. With the paddle attachment on low speed, work in the cold butter until the mixture is crumbly with pea-sized or just larger bits of butter remaining. In a small bowl or glass measure, whisk together the eggs, cream, and vanilla until frothy. With mixer on stir speed, pour cream mixture into the dry ingredients. Add tart cherries; combine. Do not overmix.

The dough will be somewhat sticky. Scoop out onto a floured surface. With floured fingertips, pat out to 1-inch [2.5 cm] thick. Using a floured 3-inch [7.5 cm] biscuit cutter or drinking glass, cut dough into circles and place onto prepared baking sheet.

Lightly brush cream on top of the scones and sprinkle with turbinado sugar if desired. Place baking sheet, uncovered, in the freezer for 15 minutes.

Remove baking sheet from freezer and bake 15-20 minutes or until golden brown. Remove from the oven and let rest on cooling rack for 5 minutes. If glazing, combine confectioner's sugar and fresh orange juice until smooth. Drizzle over scones.

EnJOY!

Variations:

Omit cherries and add mini chocolate chips, chopped pecans, fresh blueberries, fresh raspberries or cinnamon chips

INGREDIENTS

- ◆ 5 oz [142 g] GF flour blend
- ◆ 1 oz [28 g] tigernut flour or GF flour blend
- ◆ 1 1/2 oz [43 g] coconut sugar or unrefined cane sugar
- ◆ 2 tablespoons [30 ml] finely chopped orange zest
- ◆ 1 tablespoon [15 ml] baking powder
- ◆ ½ teaspoon [2.5 ml] sea salt
- ◆ ½ cup [113 g] cold, unsalted butter, diced
- ◆ ½ cup [120 ml] dried tart Montmorency cherries
- ◆ 2 pastured eggs
- ◆ ½ cup [120 ml] cold heavy cream, buttermilk, or full fat coconut milk
- ◆ 1 teaspoon [5 ml] pure vanilla, spiced rum or orange liqueur of choice
- ◆ Extra cream
- ◆ Turbinado sugar (optional)

Orange Glaze (optional)
- ◆ 2 oz [56 g] confectioner's sugar
- ◆ 1 tablespoon [15 ml] fresh orange juice

Makes 6 scones

There were several before-school mornings when I popped open a can of Pillsbury cinnamon rolls to surprise my daughter Mary. Those days are long gone and now we have a tradition of making homemade, gooey cinnamon rolls whenever we visit one another. Hope you enjoy these warm-from-the-oven rolls like we do!

FROSTING

In a medium bowl, beat butter and cream cheese until fluffy. Add confectioner's sugar, milk and vanilla; beat until light and fluffy. Spread on slightly warm or cooled rolls.

Frosting

- ♦ 3 tablespoons [42 g] salted butter, softened
- ♦ 1 oz [28 g] cream cheese, softened
- ♦ 3 oz [85 g] confectioner's sugar
- ♦ 2 teaspoons [10 ml] goat's milk or other milk of choice or cream
- ♦ 1 teaspoon [5 ml] pure vanilla

MISS MARY'S CINNAMON ROLLS

This recipe requires exact metric measurements. Doesn't the whole world use metric now anyway?

Grease a 9x13-inch [23x33-cm] baking pan or equivalent casserole dish; set aside.

DOUGH

Whisk all the dry ingredients in the bowl of a stand mixer fitted with a paddle attachment. Add the cider vinegar, butter, egg, and warm water and mix on low speed to combine. Turn to high and mix for 3 minutes more.

Turn the dough out onto a flat, lightly floured (use GF flour blend) surface. Sprinkle dough with flour as necessary, using a floured rolling pin, rolling into a rectangle (12x20 inches [30x50 cm]). Dough should be about ½-inch [13 mm] thick.

FILLING

In a small bowl, combine very soft butter and orange zest (if using). Using an offset spatula or back of spoon, spread the softened butter all around the rectangle, leaving ½-inch [13-mm] border free. In a small bowl, combine brown sugar and cinnamon. Sprinkle cinnamon sugar evenly on top of the butter, patting down gently. Starting at 12-inch [30-cm] side, roll the dough tightly into a coil. Using a piece of unwaxed dental floss or a very sharp knife, cut rolls in 2-inch [5-cm] pieces. Place rolls in the prepared baking dish, about 1 inch [2.5 cm] apart. Cover the pan with a flour sack towel and set in a warm, draft-free location to rise about 90 minutes.

When the dough is nearing the end of its rise, preheat oven to 350F [176 C]. Place the pan in the center of the preheated oven. Bake about 28-32 minutes or until the cinnamon rolls are golden brown on top and cooked in the middle. Remove from the oven and let the rolls cool. Frost as desired.

EnJOY!

Makes 10 rolls

INGREDIENTS

Dough

- 137 g sprouted brown rice flour
- 136 g white rice flour
- 68 g tapioca starch or arrowroot powder
- 68 g potato starch
- 24 g sweet potato flour or potato flour
- 9 g pectin (such as Pomona's Universal Pectin)
- 25 g psyllium husk powder
- 43 g goat milk powder
- 7 g instant yeast
- ¼ teaspoon [1.25 ml] cream of tartar
- ¼ teaspoon [1.25 ml] baking soda
- ¼ teaspoon [1.25 ml] ground cardamom
- 26 g brown sugar or coconut sugar
- 1 teaspoon [5 ml] sea salt
- 1 teaspoon [5 ml] apple cider vinegar
- 3 tablespoons [42 g] butter, at room temperature
- 1 pastured large egg at room temperature, beaten
- 1½ **cups** [360 ml] 100-110 F [37-43 C] warm water

Filling

- 5 tablespoons [70 g] salted butter, very soft
- 2 teaspoons [10 ml] finely chopped orange zest (optional)
- 3 oz [85 g] brown sugar or coconut sugar
- 1½ tablespoons [45 ml] Ceylon cinnamon

PINK TEEPEE FARMS
OTTAWA, WISCONSIN

Most of us do not forage for our food. Maybe we think of hunter and gatherer lessons from school at the mention of the word "forage." We might even wonder what in the world we would go foraging for.

Ben and Molly Wiedenman of Pink TeePee Farms know. They not only know what to forage and where to forage, they also LOVE to forage. Every spring, summer, and autumn, Molly and Ben are on a treasure hunt in Southeastern Wisconsin for exotic mushrooms, ramps, fiddleheads, and chaga.

They bring their finds to the Oconomowoc Farmer's Market, sell through their CSA, and direct wholesale to local restaurants including ID, Belfrē Ktchen, Twisted Fire, Wine Maniacs, Delafield Brewhouse, Fresh Baked, and 2894 on Main.

Besides sustainably harvesting in the wild, Ben, Molly, and their super-neighbor, friend, and colleague, Keith Alexander, grow over 50 varieties of fruits and vegetables on their property. This full-time enterprise came after growing up with family gardens and after leaving different careers behind to pursue what makes them feel alive.

Ben studied environmental science, conservation, biology, and aquaponics. In his own words he ""fell down the rabbit hole of small scale food production, farming, aquaponics, and aqua culture." Molly, who started her career as a teacher, has happily fallen as well. Together they make a vibrant team as they learn more and more every year about growing a successful agriculture business, as well as learning new crops such as hemp. Their model is found in working with Mother Nature, following the flow of the seasons, and using organic Native American practices in their farming.

There are days when Keith, Molly and Ben are drained, spent, and question their zest for the enormity of the work. Then they hear from clients whose lives have been changed by the wholesome food they get from the farm, or from chefs who delight in creating with their foraged delicacies, and the spark that lights their enthusiasm to educate and feed their community burns bright again! Plans for food-as-medicine community dinners are underway and the Waukesha County area is ready!

COCONUT FLOUR SPROUTED CORN BREAD

Preheat oven to 350 F [176 C]. Grease an 8x8-inch [20x20-cm] baking pan or line a 12-cup muffin tin with paper liners.

In a small mixing bowl, combine coconut flour, sprouted corn flour, coconut sugar, sea salt, baking powder and baking soda; set aside. In a separate medium mixing bowl, combine eggs, milk of choice and melted butter or oil; beat well. Add flour mixture and whisk until blended. Spread in prepared pan or divide evenly among 12 muffin cups.

Bake 20-24 minutes for an 8x8-inch [20x20 cm] pan or 12-15 minutes for muffins; or until tester comes out clean. Transfer baking pan to cooling rack and allow to cool at least 20 minutes before serving. For muffins, immediately remove from tin to cooling rack. Delicious with raw, local honey-butter.

EnJOY!

Variations

- Omit sugar and add 6 oz [170 g] shredded cheddar and ¼ cup [60 ml] finely sliced scallions.
- Fold in 1 cup [240 ml] fresh blueberries to batter just before filling pan or muffin cups.

INGREDIENTS

- ♦ 1 oz [28 g] coconut flour
- ♦ 3 oz [85 g] sprouted corn flour
- ♦ 1½ oz [42 g] coconut sugar
- ♦ ¼ teaspoon [1.25 ml] sea salt
- ♦ 1 teaspoon [5 ml] baking powder
- ♦ ½ teaspoon [2.5 ml] baking soda
- ♦ 4 pastured eggs, room temperature
- ♦ 1 cup [240 ml] milk of choice
- ♦ ¼ cup [60 ml] avocado oil, melted coconut oil, or melted butter

Makes one 8x8-inch [20x20 cm] pan or 12 muffins

SWEET POTATO SPROUTED OAT ROLLS

In a glass measure, dissolve sugar in warm water, sprinkle in yeast; cover and set aside to proof.

In a small mixing bowl, combine flours, chia seeds, baking soda, baking powder, and sea salt; set aside. In a separate medium bowl, combine sweet potato, honey, oil, and eggs. Beat with an electric mixer until frothy. Add proofed yeast mixture; stir to combine.

Add dry flour mixture to sweet potato mixture; stir well. Cover and allow to rest 10 minutes. Preheat oven to 350 F [176 C]. Grease a 9x13-inch [33x23-cm] pan or two 8-inch [20-cm] round pans and line with parchment paper. (A well-greased muffin top pan may also be used).

With a cookie scoop, portion batter into pans, creating equal-sized dough balls. Cover and allow to rest 25 minutes.

Bake 32-35 minutes, until rolls are deep golden. Allow to sit in pans for 5-10 minutes before removing to cooling rack.

EnJOY!

INGREDIENTS

- 2 teaspoons [10 ml] active dry yeast
- 1 teaspoon [5 ml] sugar (for proofing yeast)
- ⅔ cup [160 ml] water at 110-120 F [43-49 C]
- 8 oz [227 g] baked, peeled, and mashed sweet potato
- 4 oz [113 g] raw, local honey
- ¼ cup [60 ml] avocado oil or coconut oil, melted
- 2 pastured eggs, room temperature
- 6 oz [170 g] sprouted oat flour
- 6 oz [170 g] GF flour blend
- 1 oz [28 g] almond flour or GF flour blend
- 1 tablespoon [15 ml] chia seeds, ground if desired
- 1 teaspoon [5 ml] baking soda
- 1 teaspoon [5 ml] baking powder
- 2 teaspoons [10 ml] sea salt

Makes 12 rolls

EVERYWHERE IS LOCAL

SPROUTED BROWN RICE FLOUR PIZZA CRUST

Preheat oven to 400 F [204 C]. Cut a 12-inch [30-cm] round piece of parchment paper to line a 12-13-inch [30-33-cm] pizza pan; set aside.

In a medium bowl, whisk together the rice flour, potato starch, arrowroot, psyllium powder, sugar, yeast and sea salt. In a 2-cup [480-ml] glass measure, stir together warm water, 1 tablespoon [15 ml] olive oil, and apple cider vinegar. Pour water mixture into dry ingredients and whisk vigorously or use a hand-held electric mixer to blend ingredients until smooth.

Pour remaining 1 tablespoon [15 ml] olive oil onto the center of the parchment-lined pizza pan. With an oiled spatula, scoop dough onto olive oil in pan. With wet fingertips, gently smooth dough in circular motions to cover pan. Allow dough to rest 20 minutes.

At the end of rest time, bake crust for 18-20 minutes. Remove from oven and increase temperature to 450 F [232 C]. Top crust with desired pizza ingredients. Bake an additional 12-15 minutes.

EnJOY!

Variation

Add ½ teaspoon [2.5 ml] dried oregano or Italian spice blend to dry ingredients list.

INGREDIENTS

- 3 oz [85 g] sprouted brown rice flour
- 2 oz [56 g] potato starch
- 1 oz [28 g] arrowroot powder
- 1 teaspoon [5 ml] psyllium husk powder
- 1 teaspoon [5 ml] coconut or cane sugar
- 2 teaspoons [10 ml] active dry yeast
- 1 teaspoon [5 ml] sea salt
- ¾ cup [180 ml] 95-110 F [35-43 C] warm water
- 2 tablespoon [30 ml] olive oil (divided)
- 1 teaspoon [5 ml] apple cider vinegar

Makes one 12-inch [30-cm] pizza crust

SPROUTED BROWN RICE FLOUR NAAN

In a medium bowl, mix together the rice flour, ground flax or chia, arrowroot or tapioca, yeast, psyllium husks, and sea salt. Stir in the hot water, oil, and honey.

Cover bowl and allow dough to rest 20-25 minutes.

Heat a 9-inch [23-cm] cast-iron skillet over medium heat.

Sprinkle rice flour over counter or board for rolling dough. Divide dough into 8 equal pieces. Roll each piece very thin, about ⅛-inch [3 mm] or less. Transfer rolled dough to hot skillet by scooping onto a large spatula then flipping over from spatula to skillet.

Cook the naan until it puffs slightly and gets some dark spots (about 2 minutes). Flip and cook through, just a few minutes more. Turn heat to medium-low if naan is charring too quickly. As each naan cooks, roll out next piece of dough. Place naan on a plate under a towel until ready to serve.

EnJOY!

INGREDIENTS

♦ 5 oz [142 g] sprouted brown or white rice flour

♦ 1½ oz [45 g] golden flax meal or ground chia seeds

♦ 2 oz [56 g] arrowroot or tapioca powder

♦ 1 teaspoon [5 ml] active dry yeast

♦ 1 tablespoon [15 ml] whole psyllium husks

♦ ¾ teaspoon [7.5 ml] sea salt or garlic salt

♦ 1 cup [240 ml] 95-110 F [35-43 C] warm water

♦ 2 teaspoons [10 ml] honey or unrefined cane sugar

♦ 3 tablespoons [45 ml] avocado, olive, or melted coconut oil

♦ Additional sprouted brown or white rice flour

Serves 2 to 4

SPROUTED CHICKPEA FLOUR FLATBREAD

In a medium mixing bowl, combine flour, water, oil, sea salt, cumin, and garlic powder. Whisk until smooth, cover, and set aside 30 minutes (or up to 12 hours).

Heat oven to 450 F [232 C]. Place a well-seasoned 10-inch [25-cm] cast-iron skillet on the middle rack while oven is heating. Once oven is at temperature, remove skillet, add 2 tablespoons [30 ml] oil and swirl skillet to coat the bottom evenly. Add batter and place back in the oven for 12-15 minutes, until golden on the edges and firm throughout. If a charred finish is preferred, turn broiler to high, and broil for about 2 minutes, until top starts to get deep golden.

Remove pan and let cool a few minutes. Using a metal spatula, gently push under and around the sides of the flatbread. Tip skillet or carefully flip skillet over to remove. Garnish as desired.

Cut into slices or pull apart and eat. Sprouted chickpea flatbread is best eaten right away.

EnJOY!

INGREDIENTS

- 1 cup [240 ml] sprouted chickpea flour
- 1 cup [240 ml] lukewarm water
- 2 tablespoons [30 ml] olive oil or avocado oil, and more for pan
- ½ teaspoon [2.5 ml] sea salt
- ¼ teaspoon [1.25 ml] ground cumin
- ¼ teaspoon [1.25 ml] garlic powder
- ½ teaspoon [2.5 ml] finely chopped fresh rosemary (optional)
- Fresh cracked pepper (optional)
- Za'atar seasoning (for garnish)
- Flaky sea salt (for garnish)
- Fresh chopped flat leaf parsley (for garnish)

Makes 2 servings

COOKIES & BARS

the best time
to eat a chocolate
chip cookie?
5 minutes out
of the oven

Soft Ginger-Molasses Cookies, 153

Sweet & Salty Peanut Butter Cookies, 155

Snickerdoodles, 157

Chewy Chocolate Chip Cookies, 159

Rum- Raisin Sprouted Oatmeal Cookies, 161

Flourless Double Chocolate Brownies, 163

Strawberry-Rhubarb Sprouted Oat Crumble Bars, 165

Lemon Lavender Bars, 169

Sweet Potato Sprouted Oat Breakfast Cookies, 171

SOFT GINGER-MOLASSES COOKIES

Preheat oven to 350 F [176 C] and adjust rack to middle position. Whisk flours, cinnamon, pumpkin pie spice, baking soda, ginger, and sea salt in a large mixing bowl. Stir in egg, melted butter, honey, and molasses until combined. Chill dough for 30-60 minutes.

Using a 1-inch [2.5-cm] cookie scoop, scoop a dough ball, roll in palms and drop it into a small bowl with sugar of choice. Roll the cookie dough around to coat. Set the ball on a baking sheet lined with parchment paper. Place dough balls about 1½-inches [4 cm] apart. Bake 9-10 minutes. Cool on rack for 10 minutes.

EnJOY!

INGREDIENTS

- 8 oz [227 g] finely ground almond flour
- 1 oz [28 g] arrowroot flour, tapioca starch or cornstarch
- 1 oz [28 g] coconut flour
- 1 teaspoon [5 ml] ground Ceylon cinnamon
- 1 teaspoon [5 ml] pumpkin pie spice (or additional Ceylon cinnamon)
- 1 tablespoon [15 ml] baking soda
- 1 teaspoon [5 ml] ground ginger
- ½ teaspoon [2.5 ml] sea salt
- 1 pastured egg, gently beaten
- 8 tablespoons [113 g] unsalted butter or shortening, melted
- ⅓ cup [80 ml] raw, local honey
- ⅓ cup [80 ml] unsulphured molasses
- Granulated sugar, maple sugar, or coconut sugar for rolling

Makes 45 2-inch [5-cm] cookies

SWEET & SALTY PEANUT BUTTER COOKIES

Heat oven to 325 F [163 C] and line 2 baking sheets with parchment paper. In a stand mixer fitted with a paddle attachment, or using a hand-held electric mixer, cream the butter and sugars until smooth and fluffy, 3-4 minutes. Add the peanut butter (and NuttZo if using—see Variation below) and egg; mix to combine. Add the flour and sea salt and stir just until combined.

Using a 2-inch [5 cm] cookie scoop, scoop dough onto prepared pans. You may either leave the dough rounded or press slightly with palm. The cookies will not spread much when they bake, so they can be placed about 1 inch [2.5 cm] apart.

In a small bowl, mix 1 tablespoon [15 ml] sugar with ½ tablespoon [7 ml] flaky salt. Sprinkle each cookie lightly with sugar-salt mixture. Bake 14-15 minutes, until cookies are set and golden. Set pan on cooling racks or slide off parchment paper onto cooling racks.

EnJOY!

Variation:

You may substitute half the peanut butter for a seed and nut blend called Nuttzo. It's delicious and includes cashews, almonds, Brazil nuts, flax seeds, chia seeds, hazelnuts, and pumpkin seeds.

INGREDIENTS

- ♦ ½ cup [113g] unsalted butter, softened (if you can find cultured butter, all the better!)
- ♦ 2½ oz [75 g] granulated sugar
- ♦ 3 oz [85 g] brown sugar
- ♦ ½ teaspoon [2.5 ml] sea salt
- ♦ 8 oz [250 g] unsweetened peanut butter, creamy or chunky
- ♦ 1 pastured egg, room temperature
- ♦ 2½ oz [75 g] finely ground almond flour
- ♦ 1¾ oz [50 g] GF flour blend
- ♦ Flaky sea salt (Maldon) and coarse or regular granulated sugar for cookie tops

Makes 20-21 2-inch [5-cm] cookies

SNICKERDOODLES

Preheat oven to 350 F [176 C]. Line 2 baking sheets with parchment paper; set aside.

In a medium bowl, using an electric mixer, beat sugar of choice and egg for 2 minutes. Add melted butter; beat well. Add honey and vanilla; beat well.

In a separate small mixing bowl, blend almond flour, GF flour, collagen powder (if using), baking soda, cream of tartar, and sea salt.

Mix again on stir speed until dough forms. Cover and chill for 20-30 minutes.

Combine cinnamon and sugar of choice in a shallow bowl.

Using a 1-inch [2.5-cm] dough scoop, scoop dough into balls, then roll in cinnamon-sugar mixture. Place dough balls 2 inches [5 cm] apart on prepared baking sheets.

Bake for 10-12 minutes until lightly golden. Transfer cookies to a wire rack to cool completely.

EnJOY!

INGREDIENTS

- 3½ oz [100 g] coconut or cane sugar
- 1 pastured egg, room temperature
- 6 tablespoons [85 g] butter, ghee, or coconut oil; melted and slightly cooled
- 2 tablespoons [30 ml] raw, local honey
- 1 teaspoon [5 ml] pure vanilla
- 4 oz [96 g] almond flour
- 5 oz [142 g] GF flour blend
- 1 tablespoon [15 ml] multi-collagen powder (optional)
- ½ teaspoon [2.5 ml] baking soda
- ½ teaspoon [2.5 ml] cream of tartar
- ⅛ teaspoon [.6 ml] sea salt
- 1 teaspoon [5 ml] Ceylon cinnamon
- 2 tablespoons [30 ml] coconut or cane sugar

Makes about one dozen cookies

CHEWY CHOCOLATE CHIP COOKIES

Preheat oven to 350 F [176 C]. Cream egg, cream cheese, butter, coconut or brown sugar, and vanilla (and almond extract if using) in a medium mixing bowl or 8-cup [2-liter] glass measure.

In a separate bowl, combine dry ingredients except chocolate chips. Stir flour mixture into creamed mixture. Fold in chocolate chips. Chill 30 minutes.

Using a medium (1-inch [2.5 cm]) cookie scoop, form cookie dough balls and place 2 inches [5 cm] apart on parchment-lined baking sheet. Bake 12-14 minutes. Sprinkle with flaky sea salt if desired. Allow cookies to cool on baking sheet for about 5 minutes before serving.

EnJOY!

Add-ins:

- 1½ oz [46 g] finely shredded unsweetened coconut
- 2½ oz [70 g] dried tart cherries, chopped if desired
- 2 oz [60 g] coarsely chopped walnuts or pecans

INGREDIENTS

- 1 pastured egg, room temperature
- ½ oz [14 g] cream cheese, room temperature
- 5 tablespoons [70 g] unsalted butter, soft
- 5 oz [142 g] coconut sugar or brown sugar (light or dark)
- 2 teaspoons [10 ml] pure vanilla
- 1 teaspoon [5 ml] almond extract (optional)
- 3 oz [85 g] almond flour
- 4 oz [113 g] GF flour blend
- ¼ teaspoon [1.25 ml] guar powder (optional)
- ½ teaspoon [2.5 ml] baking soda
- ½ teaspoon [2.5 ml] sea salt
- 3 oz [85 g] chocolate chips or chocolate chunks of choice
- Flaky sea salt (optional for cookie tops)

Makes 18 to 20 cookies

RUM-RAISIN SPROUTED OATMEAL COOKIES

In a small dish, combine raisins, rum, and orange zest. Allow to rest 1 hour.

Preheat oven to 325 F [162 C]. Line two baking sheets with parchment paper; set aside. In a medium bowl or 8-cup [2-liter] glass measure, beat butter and sugars until light and creamy; about 2 minutes. Add eggs; beat well.

In a separate bowl, combine flours, baking soda, sea salt, and spices. Add to wet ingredients; stir to combine. Stir in oats and soaked raisins (with liquid). Using a 2-oz [60-ml] cookie scoop, scoop dough balls onto prepared baking sheets. Bake 10-12 minutes until golden brown. Cool 5 minutes before removing to cooling rack.

Best if eaten day of bake.

EnJOY!

Variations:

♦ Substitute chopped tart cherries for raisins and ½ teaspoon [5 ml] almond extract or orange liqueur for spiced rum.

♦ Omit soaked, dried fruit altogether and add ½ teaspoon vanilla to the batter.

INGREDIENTS

♦ 1½ oz [43 g] raisins, finely chopped

♦ 2 tablespoons [30 ml] spiced rum

♦ 2 teaspoons [10 ml] blood orange or regular orange zest, finely chopped

♦ ½ cup [113 g] unsalted butter, soft

♦ 4 oz [113 g] cane or coconut sugar

♦ 1 pastured egg, room temperature

♦ 1 oz [28 g] GF flour blend

♦ 2 oz [56 g] finely ground almond flour or GF flour blend

♦ ½ teaspoon [2.5 ml] baking soda

♦ ¼ teaspoon [1.25 ml] sea salt

♦ ¾ teaspoon [3.75 ml] Ceylon cinnamon

♦ ¼ teaspoon [1.25] cardamom

♦ ⅛ teaspoon [.6 ml] nutmeg

♦ 5 1/2 oz [156 g] sprouted old-fashioned rolled oats

Makes about 16 cookies

FLOURLESS DOUBLE CHOCOLATE BROWNIES

Preheat oven to 350 F [176 C]. Grease and line an 8x8-inch [20x20-cm] baking pan with parchment paper, covering bottom and up sides, leaving enough extra paper for easy brownie removal.

Combine coconut oil and butter in a small saucepan. Heat over medium-low heat until butter begins to bubble. Remove from heat and add chocolate chips, swirling pan to cover chocolate chips with butter-oil; set aside.

Using a hand-held mixer or a stand mixer with a whisk attachment, beat eggs, sugar, and vanilla until smooth and fluffy, about 3 minutes. Stir chocolate in pan until homogenized with the butter-oil. Pour chocolate into egg-sugar mixture, scraping out pan with a rubber spatula, and beat for one minute.

Add cacao powder, arrowroot powder, and sea salt to chocolate mixture. With a rubber spatula, fold dry ingredients gently into batter for several turns. Finish combining with an electric or stand mixer on medium speed.

Spread batter into prepared pan. Bake 24 minutes. Remove pan to cooling rack for 20 minutes. Remove brownies from pan using parchment paper handles. Allow to cool completely. Cut into squares.

EnJOY!

Variations:

- Add up to 1 cup chopped pecans or walnuts to batter before baking.
- Add 1 tablespoon [15 ml] instant coffee to batter before baking.
- Add 1 teaspoon [5 ml] pure peppermint extract or 3 drops oil of peppermint to batter before baking.
- Frost with vanilla, chocolate, or peanut butter frosting.

INGREDIENTS

- 3 tablespoons [45 ml] coconut oil, melted
- 3 tablespoons [42 g] unsalted butter, melted
- 6 oz [170 g] dark or semi-sweet chocolate chips
- 2 pastured eggs, room temperature
- 5 oz [150 g] coconut or cane sugar
- 2 teaspoons [10 ml] pure vanilla
- 1¼ oz [35 g] raw cacao powder
- 1½ oz [43 g] arrowroot powder
- ¼ teaspoon [1.25 ml] sea salt

Makes one 8x8-inch [20x20 cm] pan

STRAWBERRY-RHUBARB SPROUTED OAT CRUMBLE BARS

Preheat oven to 350 degrees F [176 C]. Grease and line an 8x8-inch [20x20-cm] pan with parchment paper with sides for lifting out; set aside.

CRUST

Add oats, almonds, sea salt, and coconut sugar to a food processor or high-speed blender and pulse into a fine meal. Add melted coconut oil and pulse to incorporate until a loose dough forms when squeezed between fingers. (Add more melted oil if too dry.) Spread the mixture into the prepared pan and press down into an even layer with your fingers or the bottom of a drinking glass. Bake 20 minutes, or until the crust is fragrant and the edges are slightly golden brown. Remove from oven and set aside.

FILLING

Combine rhubarb, strawberries, orange juice, coconut sugar, and arrowroot in a medium saucepan and cook over medium-low heat until fruit is slightly softened and bubbly, about 7-8 minutes. (Stir frequently to prevent sticking.) Remove from heat and set aside.

CRUMBLE TOPPING

Combine all topping ingredients in a small mixing bowl using a fork or your fingers to mix ingredients into a crumble; set aside.

Spread strawberry-rhubarb mixture in an even layer on the pre-baked crust. Top with crumble topping, spreading evenly to cover fruit. Bake 15-20 minutes or until the strawberry topping is warm and bubbly and the crumble is golden brown. Remove from oven and let cool completely on cooling rack, 1-2 hours.

EnJOY!

INGREDIENTS

Crust

- 3 oz [85 g] sprouted rolled oats
- 8 oz [226 g] sprouted almonds
- ¼ teaspoon [1.25 ml] sea salt
- 2 oz [56 g] coconut sugar or brown cane sugar
- 4 tablespoons [60 ml] melted coconut oil or melted butter

Filling

- 8 oz [226 g] rhubarb, chopped into small pieces
- 15 oz [425 g] strawberries, chopped
- ¼ cup [60 ml] fresh orange juice
- 2 oz [56 g] coconut sugar or cane sugar
- ¼ oz [7 g] arrowroot powder or cornstarch

Crumble Topping

- 2 oz [56 g] coconut sugar or brown cane sugar
- ½ oz [14 g] GF flour blend
- 1 oz [28 g] sprouted rolled oats
- 1 oz [28 g] sliced almonds
- 2 tablespoons [30 ml] coconut oil or melted butter

Makes one 8x8–inch [20x20-cm] pan

JAM SESSIONS JAM CAMBRIDGE, MASSACHUSETTS

I would like you to meet Afton Cyrus. She is the quintessential story of how one must look inward for illumination when following a passion.

Afton grew up in Maine, where she first learned to can and preserve food from her family's garden as a teenager. Even after moving to Cambridge, MA to pursue a master's in music and education from Harvard University, she continued to can her own jams, pickles, and fruit preserves every summer. This hard work with summer's bounty supported her growing love of food and cooking. As Afton began to forge relationships with farms in the area, she became passionate about local business, seasonal eating, and sustainable agriculture.

By 2014, some chapters in Afton's life were closing and leading her to a crossroads. She began to ask herself some penetrating questions about what brought her joy, what fueled her creative life, and how would she like to see her journey forward. She decided to bring her love of cooking with local food to the forefront, and channeled her artistic energy into a new pursuit, bravely leaving a 10-year career behind, and launched Jam Sessions. Through her venture, she aims to delight her customers with unique and exceptional flavor combinations of jams and jellies, highlighting wonderful local New England farm produce.

By following her inspiration, her work with Jam Sessions led to an additional new career as a Test Cook and author at America's Test Kitchen, where she develops recipes for cookbooks by day, (including the great canning resource, *Foolproof Preserving*), and jams by night, sharing her wares at Boston-area farmer's markets.

LEMON LAVENDER BARS

Preheat oven to 325 F [163 C]. Grease and line an 8x8-inch [20x20-cm] baking pan with parchment paper; overhanging for easy removal. Set aside.

CRUST

In the bowl of a food processor, add flours, sugar, coconut, sea salt, lavender or thyme, cinnamon, and nutmeg. Pulse until all ingredients are well blended. With processor running, slowing pour in melted butter until a soft, crumbly dough forms.

Spread the dough evenly on the bottom of the prepared baking pan. Bake 15 minutes until crust is just golden. Remove from oven and set aside.

FILLING

Combine lemon zest, juice, and sugar in the bowl of a food processor. Blend for 3 minutes. With the processor running, add the butter little by little. Add the eggs, sea salt, and arrowroot powder. Blend until light and fluffy, about 2-3 minutes.

Carefully pour the lemon filling over the crust and bake 35-37 minutes until edges are lightly golden and center is barely set. Cool in the pan for at least two hours. Move bars to refrigerator to chill completely. Cut and sprinkle with confectioner's sugar as desired.

EnJOY!

INGREDIENTS

Crust

- 6 tablespoons [85 g] unsalted butter, melted and cooled
- 2 oz [56 g] finely ground almond flour or 2½ oz [72 g] GF flour blend
- 2½ oz [72 g] GF flour blend
- 2 oz [56 g] cane or coconut sugar
- ¼ oz [14 g] unsweetened shredded coconut
- ¼ teaspoon [1.25 ml] smoked or regular sea salt
- 1 teaspoon [5 ml] dried organic lavender buds or fresh lemon thyme leaves (or both, or none)
- ¼ teaspoon [1.25 ml] Ceylon cinnamon
- Pinch nutmeg

Filling

- 1 tablespoon [15 ml] fresh lemon zest, chopped finely
- ½ cup [120 ml] fresh lemon juice
- 7 oz [200 g] cane sugar
- 8 tablespoons [113 g] unsalted butter, cut into small cubes or slices
- 4 pastured eggs, room temperature
- 1 oz [28 g] arrowroot powder or cornstarch
- ¼ teaspoon [1.25 ml] sea salt or red algae salt
- Confectioner's sugar for dusting (optional)

Makes one 8x8 [20x20 cm] pan

SWEET POTATO SPROUTED BREAKFAST COOKIES

Preheat oven to 325 F [163 C]. Line baking sheet with parchment paper; set aside.

In a large mixing bowl, combine oats, oat flour, dried cranberries, pumpkin seeds, collagen powder (if using), flaxseed meal, chia seeds, cinnamon, baking powder, and sea salt.

In a small bowl, whisk the mashed sweet potato, coconut oil, pure maple syrup, and cream or milk of choice until well blended. Combine wet and dry mixtures. Allow mixture to rest for 4–5 minutes. If the dough becomes too thick, stir in an additional 1–2 tablespoons [15-30 ml] cream or milk before scooping out onto your baking sheet.

Using a ¼-cup [60-ml] dough scoop, scoop batter onto the prepared baking sheet. Gently press each dough ball with fingers or bottom of drinking glass to flatten a bit.

Bake for 18-20 minutes, or until cookies are lightly golden around the edges. Remove to cooling rack. Serve warm if desired.

EnJOY!

INGREDIENTS

- 3 oz [85 g] sprouted rolled oats
- 1 oz [28 g] sprouted oat flour (you can make your own in a food processor)
- 1 oz [28 g] dried cranberries or tart cherries, chopped
- 1 oz [28 g] sprouted pumpkin seeds
- 1 oz [28 g] multi-collagen powder (optional)
- ¼ oz [7 g] golden flaxseed meal
- ½ oz [14 g] chia seeds
- 2 teaspoons [10 ml] Ceylon cinnamon
- ½ teaspoon [2.5 ml] baking powder
- ¼ teaspoon [1.25 ml] sea salt
- 2 oz [56 g] cooked mashed sweet potato (or banana)
- 4 tablespoons [60 ml] melted coconut oil, melted butter, or melted ghee
- 4 tablespoons [60 ml] pure maple syrup, local honey, or coconut nectar
- 4 tablespoons [60 ml] heavy cream, almond milk, or other milk of choice

Makes 12 cookies

CAKES & CUPCAKES

Every day is a special occasion

Hummingbird Cake, 177

Deep Chocolate Cake with French Buttercream, 179

Flourless Hazelnut Fudge Cake, 181

Catherine's Carrot Cake, 183

Meyer Lemon Poppyseed Cake, 187

Vanilla-Amaretto Bundt Cake, 189

Sweet Potato Sprouted Oat Crumb Cupcakes, 191

Pumpkin Cake Bars, 193

Yerba Mate Banana Snack Cake, 195

HUMMINGBIRD CAKE

Preheat oven to 325 F [163C]. Grease two 8-inch [20-cm] cake pans and line bottoms with parchment paper; set aside.

Place all cake ingredients into a large mixing bowl and whisk or beat with electric mixer until combined. Allow to rest 5 minutes. Divide batter between the two prepared cake pans. Smooth the top of the batter with a rubber or offset spatula.

Bake for 30-32 minutes or until the center is set and edges pull away from the sides of the pan. Remove from the oven and let cake layers cool for 10 minutes in pans before removing to a wire rack to cool completely.

While cake is baking, beat butter and cream cheese together in medium bowl until fluffy. Add maple syrup and vanilla; beat well and set aside. Once cake is cool, frost the tops and stack them. Smooth a light layer of frosting on sides. Garnish with chopped pecans or walnuts as desired.

EnJOY!

INGREDIENTS

Cake

- ♦ 2 medium overripe bananas, mashed
- ♦ ¼ cup [60 ml] avocado oil or melted coconut oil
- ♦ ½ cup [120 ml] pure maple syrup or local raw honey
- ♦ 4 pastured eggs, room temperature
- ♦ 1 cup [240 ml] finely minced fresh pineapple or canned crushed pineapple, lightly drained
- ♦ 1 tablespoon [15 ml] rum, grand marnier, or pure vanilla extract
- ♦ 12 oz [340 g] finely ground almond flour
- ♦ ½ oz [14 g] arrowroot or tapioca powder
- ♦ ½ teaspoon [2.5 ml] sea salt
- ♦ 1 teaspoon [5 ml] Ceylon cinnamon
- ♦ 2 teaspoons [10 ml] baking soda
- ♦ 2 oz [56 g] toasted pecans or walnuts, chopped
- ♦ Toasted pecans or walnuts for garnish (optional)

Maple Cream Cheese Frosting

- ♦ ½ cup [113 g] salted butter, room temperature
- ♦ 8 oz [227 g] cream cheese, room temperature
- ♦ ¼ cup [60 ml] pure maple syrup
- ♦ 1 teaspoon [5 ml] pure vanilla extract
- ♦ 4 cups lightly sweetened whipped cream (dairy or coconut)

Makes one 2-layer, 8-inch [20-cm] cake

DEEP CHOCOLATE CAKE WITH FRENCH BUTTERCREAM FROSTING

Preheat oven to 325 F [163 C]. Grease two 8-inch [20-cm] cake pans and line bottoms with parchment paper; set aside. For cupcakes, line muffin tins with paper liners; set aside.

Place all dry cake ingredients into a large mixing bowl and whisk or beat with electric mixer until combined. In a separate large mixing bowl, beat oil, eggs, syrup and vanilla together until frothy. Pour into dry ingredients and stir until combined. Allow to rest 5 minutes. Divide batter between the two prepared cake pans or into paper cupcake liners.

Bake for 28-32 minutes or until the center is set and edges pull away from the sides of the pan. For cupcakes, bake 22-25 minutes until cupcake top springs back slightly when touched. For cake, remove from the oven and let cake layers cool for 10 minutes in pans before removing to a wire rack to cool completely. For cupcakes, remove from tins to wire racks immediately.

WHILE CAKE IS BAKING, MAKE FRENCH BUTTERCREAM FROSTING:

In a heavy, stainless steel saucepan, combine water, sugar, and cream of tartar. Place over high heat. Put yolks and egg in a stand mixer with the whisk attachment and whip on high speed. While eggs are beating, bring sugar mixture in pan on stove to 235 F [113 C] or soft ball stage.

Moving quickly, turn mixer to medium-low speed, then rest the lip of the saucepan on the edge of the mixer bowl. Slowly tilt the pan and pour the hot sugar syrup in a slow and steady stream down the side of the bowl. Once sugar is all in, turn the mixer to high again. Beat until the mixer bowl is no longer hot (will feel slightly warm-room temperature). This may take 10-15 minutes.

Switch out the whisk for the paddle attachment. Cut the butter into thin pieces or shave it with a cheese slicer. Add butter piece by piece to the bowl while paddle is beating at medium-high speed. Once all the butter is in and the frosting is smooth, add vanilla (add cacao if making chocolate frosting). Once cake is cool, spread or pipe frosting as desired.

EnJOY!

Makes one two-layer 8-inch [20 cm] cake or 16-20 cupcakes

INGREDIENTS

Cake

♦ 6 oz [170 g] finely ground almond flour
♦ 1½ oz [42 g] coconut flour
♦ 3 oz [85 g] arrowroot or tapioca powder
♦ 1½ oz [42 g] raw cacao powder
♦ 2 teaspoons [10 ml] instant coffee powder (optional)
♦ 1½ teaspoons [7.5 ml] baking soda
♦ ¾ teaspoon [3.75 ml] sea salt
♦ ¾ cup [180 ml] avocado oil or coconut oil, melted
♦ 6 pastured eggs, room temperature
♦ 1½ cup [300 ml] pure maple syrup or golden syrup
♦ 2 teaspoons [10 ml] vanilla or Amaretto liqueur

Buttercream Frosting

♦ 10½ oz [300 g] cane sugar
♦ ¾ cup [180 ml] water
♦ ⅛ teaspoon [.6 ml] cream of tartar
♦ 4 pastured egg yolks
♦ 1 pastured egg
♦ 1½ cups [339 g] cold unsalted butter
♦ ½ cup [113 g] cold salted butter
♦ 1 tablespoon [15 ml] pure vanilla

Option: 1 oz [25 g] raw cacao powder (for chocolate frosting)

Candy thermometer

FLOURLESS HAZELNUT FUDGE CAKE

Preheat to 350 F [176 C]. Butter a 9-inch [23-cm] springform pan and line bottom of pan with parchment paper. Wrap outside of pan tightly with 3 layers of recycled, heavy-duty foil; set aside.

Combine chocolate chips and butter in medium metal bowl and set bowl over saucepan of simmering water. Whisk until chocolate mixture is melted and smooth. Remove bowl from over water; set aside.

Whisk eggs, brown sugar, and ¼ cup [60 ml] Frangelico in large bowl. Add chocolate mixture and whisk until smooth. Stir in ground hazelnuts and 1 teaspoon [5 ml] coarse sea salt. Transfer batter to prepared pan.

Place springform pan in large roasting pan. Pour enough hot water into roasting pan to come halfway up sides of spring-form pan. Place in oven and tent springform pan loosely with foil. Bake until cake is set in center and top is dry to touch, about 1½ hours (top of cake will remain shiny). Remove springform pan from roasting pan; remove foil from top and outside of pan. Cool cake in pan on rack for 1 hour, then chill cake until cold, about 3 hours. (Cake can be made up to 3 days ahead. Cover and keep chilled.)

Run knife around pan sides to loosen cake. Release pan sides and place on serving platter. Using an electric mixer or stand mixer, beat whipping cream, ¼ cup [60 ml] Frangelico, and confectioner's sugar (if using) in medium bowl until soft peaks form. Pipe whipped cream or dollop onto individual servings. Decorate cake with fresh berries or sprinkle with chopped toasted hazelnuts as desired.

EnJOY!

INGREDIENTS

Cake
- 12 oz [340 g] semi-sweet or dark chocolate chips
- ¾ cup [170 g] unsalted butter, cut into chunks
- 6 pastured eggs, room temperature
- 7 oz [198 g] brown cane or coconut sugar
- ¼ cup [60 ml] Frangelico or other hazelnut liqueur
- 5 oz [142 g] finely ground hazelnuts
- 1 teaspoon [5 ml] coarse sea salt

Kettle of boiling water

Whipped Cream
- ¼ cup Frangelico or other hazelnut liqueur
- 1 cup [240 ml] chilled heavy whipping cream
- 1 oz [28 g] confectioner's sugar (optional)

Garnish
- Chopped toasted hazelnuts (optional)
- Fresh berries (optional)

Makes 12 servings

CATHERINE'S CARROT CAKE

This recipe was born when my oldest daughter, Catherine, was home visiting for her birthday and requested a gluten-free carrot cake. Although this cake feels like a special occasion, you could enjoy it any time.

CAKE

Preheat oven to 325 F [163 C]. Grease two 8-inch round cake pans and line bottoms with parchment paper; set aside.

Whisk flours, sea salt, baking powder, cardamom, cinnamon, ginger, and baking soda in a medium bowl; set aside. Using an electric mixer on medium-high speed, beat eggs and sugar in a large bowl until more than triple in volume, 7–8 minutes. Beat in vanilla.

Combine carrots, coconut, walnuts, and oil in another medium bowl. Add flour mixture in 3 additions, alternating with carrot mixture in 3 additions, to egg mixture, beating well after each addition.

Divide batter between prepared pans. Bake cake until lightly browned and a tester inserted into the center comes out clean. The top should spring back when gently poked, 35–40 minutes. Let cool 10 minutes. Carefully run a knife around edges of pans to release cake, then invert onto a wire rack. Let cool completely.

MAPLE CREAM CHEESE FROSTING

Beat cream cheese and butter until light and fluffy. Stir in remaining ingredients and beat again until light and fluffy. Frost cake and drizzle with caramel topping (optional).

EnJOY!

Makes two 8-inch [20 cm] cakes (photo depicts half recipe: single layer cake)

INGREDIENTS

Cake

- 9 oz [255 g] finely ground almond flour
- 2 oz [56 g] GF flour blend
- 1 teaspoon [5 ml] sea salt
- 1 teaspoon [5 ml] baking powder
- ½ teaspoon [2.5 ml] ground cardamom
- 1 teaspoon [5 ml] ground Ceylon cinnamon
- 1 teaspoon [5 ml] ground ginger
- ½ teaspoon [2.5 ml] baking soda
- 6 pastured eggs
- 8 oz [227 g] coconut sugar, brown sugar, or monk fruit sweetener
- ½ cup [120 ml] avocado oil or melted coconut oil
- 2 teaspoons [10 ml] pure vanilla or 1 tablespoon [15 ml] rum
- 10 oz [284 g] peeled and coarsely shredded carrots
- 2 oz [56 g] shredded unsweetened coconut
- 2 oz [56 g] walnuts, finely chopped

Maple Cream Cheese Frosting

- 8 oz [226 g] cream cheese, room temperature (or almond milk cream cheese)
- ½ cup [113 g] salted butter, room temperature (or vegan butter alternative)
- 2 oz [56 g] confectioner's sugar
- ¼ cup [60 ml] pure maple syrup
- 2 teaspoons [10 ml] pure vanilla

INYONI FARM,
NAPLES, FLORIDA

To be honest, I was surprised to find an organic farm in Naples, Florida. With its endless manicured boulevards and gated communities, who knew there was a little slice of small organic farm heaven right in its midst? Enter Nick and Natalie Batty of Inyoni Farm.

The evolution of Nick's creation of Inyoni (Swahili for "bird") began first as a young man growing up on a pineapple farm, followed by obtaining a degree in horticulture , then realizing that bringing people healthy, pesticide-free food was a good choice for him. He likes being able to provide fresh and deli-cious produce that does not require shipping and embraces an open-door policy.

Inyoni welcomes visitors to come see how they grow the food they bring to market and Nick and Natalie appreciate the dedicated clientele who frequent the Naples Farmer's Market, making them sell out every Saturday. They recognize the im-portance of connection with their community and host farm-to-table dinners with Chef Christina of Purple Spoon.

Nick and Natalie's vision for expansion is anchored more in efficient and wise farm management than in more acreage. While they currently grow about 30 varieties of lettuces, greens, herbs and fruits, they are always experimenting with new cultivars that respond well in a hot climate. Their ability to learn and adapt makes their produce some of the very best in southwestern Florida.

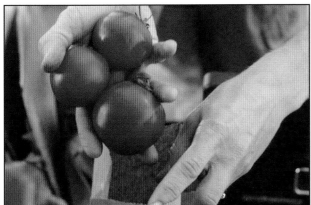

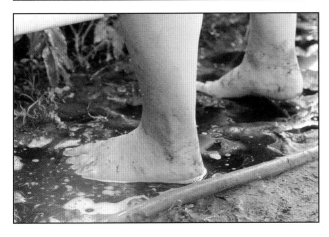

MEYER LEMON POPPY SEED CAKE

Preheat oven to 325 F [163 C]. Grease and line two 2½x5-inch [6x12 cm] mini loaf pans with parchment paper up long sides of pans.

In a medium bowl, combine the almond flour, arrowroot, coconut flour, baking powder, sea salt, and poppy seeds; set aside. In a small bowl, combine the sugar and lemon zest. Using the back of a spoon, smash zest into sugar until fragrant.

In a large bowl, whisk together the eggs, lemon juice, avocado oil, yogurt, and both extracts until well combined. Whisk in sugar-zest mixture until frothy. Gently stir the dry mixture into the wet until just combined. Divide the batter evenly between the two loaf pans.

Bake 43-45 minutes until lightly golden and tester comes out clean. Cool in pans 5 minutes and then remove to cooling rack to cool completely. Whisk together Lemon-Honey Glaze ingredients and drizzle over cooled loaves.

EnJOY!

INGREDIENTS

Cake

- 2 pastured eggs, room temperature
- 3 Meyer lemons (or regular lemons, oranges or grapefruit), zested and juiced (¼ cup [60 ml] fresh juice)
- 3 oz [85 g] cane sugar, coconut sugar, or monk fruit
- 2 tablespoons [30 ml] avocado oil or coconut oil, melted
- 1 tablespoon [15 ml] plain yogurt of choice or sour cream of choice
- 1 teaspoon [5 ml] pure vanilla
- ½ teaspoon [2.5 ml] pure almond extract
- 4 oz [113 g] finely ground almond flour
- 1 oz [28 g] arrowroot or tapioca powder
- ¼ oz [7 g] coconut flour
- 1 teaspoon [5 ml] baking powder
- ¼ teaspoon [1.25 ml] sea salt
- 1 tablespoon [15 ml] poppy seeds

Lemon-Honey Glaze

- 2 tablespoons [30 ml] liquid local honey
- 1 teaspoon [5 ml] fresh lemon juice
- ¼ teaspoon [1.25 ml] finely minced lemon zest

Makes two mini loaves

VANILLA-AMARETTO BUNDT CAKE

Preheat oven to 325 F [163 C] Thoroughly grease a standard 10-cup [2.8-liter] Bundt pan; set aside.

In a large bowl, combine GF flour blend, almond flour, sea salt, and baking powder; set aside.

In the bowl of stand mixer or a large mixing bowl with an electric mixer, cream butter, sugar, oil, vanilla and Amaretto until light and fluffy (6-7 minutes). Scrape the bowl with a rubber spatula. Beat in the eggs one at a time until fluffy and light. Scrape bowl again and beat briefly.

Fold in the milk alternately with the flour blend, one-third at a time. Scrape the bowl once more and stir thoroughly. Scoop the batter into the prepared pan.

Bake the cake for 55-60 minutes until golden brown and tester comes out clean. The cake's internal temperature should be 210 F [99 C] or higher. Cool in pan for 15 minutes before inverting onto a cooling rack.

Whisk the glaze ingredients together and drizzle over cooled cake.

EnJOY!

INGREDIENTS

Cake

- 8 oz [225 g] GF flour blend
- 6 oz [165 g] almond flour or GF flour blend
- 1 teaspoon [5 ml] sea salt
- 2 teaspoons [10 ml] baking powder
- 11½ oz [325 g] cane sugar or coconut sugar
- ½ cup [113 g] unsalted butter, softened
- 2 tablespoons [30 ml] avocado oil
- 1 tablespoon [15 ml] pure vanilla
- 1 tablespoon [15 ml] amaretto or 1 teaspoon [5 ml] pure almond extract
- 4 pastured eggs, room temperature
- ¾ cup [180 ml] buttermilk or other milk of choice, room temperature

Glaze

- 4 oz [113 g] confectioner's sugar, sifted
- 2 teaspoons [10 ml] Amaretto or ¼ teaspoon [1.25 ml] pure almond extract or 1 teaspoon [5 ml] vanilla
- 2-3 tablespoons [30-45 ml] heavy cream or full-fat coconut milk

Makes 16—20 servings

SWEET POTATO SPROUTED OAT CRUMB CUPCAKES

Preheat oven to 325 F [163 C]. Place 10 paper liners in a muffin tin; set aside.

In a small bowl, combine crumb topping ingredients; cover and chill in freezer.

In a medium bowl, combine oat flour, almond flour, baking soda, baking powder, sea salt, cinnamon, ginger, and nutmeg. In a separate medium bowl or 8-cup [2-liter] glass, measure, beat together sweet potato, eggs, maple syrup, and melted butter with an electric mixer. Pour dry ingredients into wet and stir just until combined.

Divide batter evenly between 10 prepared muffin cups. Divide crumb topping evenly over batter; pressing down slightly.

Bake 28 minutes (until tester comes out clean). Remove cakes from tin immediately to cooling rack.

EnJOY!

Makes 10 cupcakes

INGREDIENTS

Cupcakes

- 3 oz [85 g] sprouted oat flour (you can grind your own in a high-speed blender or food processor)
- 3 oz [85 g] finely ground almond flour or GF flour blend
- 1 oz [28 g] GF flour blend or arrowroot powder
- 1 teaspoon [5 ml] baking soda
- 1 teaspoon [5 ml] baking powder
- ½ teaspoon [2.5 ml] sea salt
- 1½ teaspoons [7.5 ml] Ceylon cinnamon
- ½ teaspoon [2.5 ml] ground ginger
- ¼ teaspoon [1.25 ml] ground nutmeg
- 1 cup [240 ml] baked, peeled, and puréed sweet potato
- 2 pastured eggs, room temperature
- ½ cup [120 ml] pure maple syrup
- 6 tablespoons [90 ml] melted butter, melted ghee, or melted coconut oil

Crumb Topping

- 1 oz [28 g] sprouted oat flour or almond flour
- 1 oz [28 g] coconut sugar or brown cane sugar
- ¼ oz [7 g] shredded unsweetened coconut
- 2 tablespoons [30 ml] melted butter, melted ghee, or melted coconut oil

PUMPKIN CAKE BARS

CAKE

Preheat the oven to 325 F [163 C]. Grease and line a 9x13-inch [23x33-cm] baking pan with parchment paper.

With an electric hand-held or stand mixer, beat the oil, and the sugar together until well blended. Add eggs and pumpkin purée; beat well.

Stir the baking soda, baking powder, sea salt, and spices into the wet ingredients. Add the flours, beating gently to combine. Stir in the nuts, if using. Allow the batter to rest for 15 minutes, then stir again to combine before pouring it into the prepared pan.

Bake 28-32 minutes, or until a cake tester or toothpick inserted into the middle of the cake comes out clean. Cool the cake in the pan for 10 minutes, then turn it onto a cooling rack to cool completely.

FROSTING

Beat the cream cheese until fluffy. Add butter and beat again until fluffy. Add maple syrup and vanilla; beat until well combined.

EnJOY!

INGREDIENTS

Cake

♦ ⅔ cup [158 ml] avocado oil, melted coconut oil, or olive oil

♦ 7 oz [198 g] coconut sugar or brown cane sugar

♦ 4 pastured eggs, room temperature

♦ 5 oz [150 g] pumpkin purée

♦ ¾ teaspoon [3.75 ml] baking powder

♦ ¾ teaspoon [3.75 ml] baking soda

♦ 4 oz [113 g] almond flour or GF flour blend

♦ 1½ oz [40 g] GF flour blend

♦ ½ teaspoon [2.5 ml] sea salt

♦ 2 teaspoons [10 ml] pumpkin pie spice

♦ ½ teaspoon [2.5 ml] Ceylon cinnamon

♦ ½ cup [120 ml] chopped toasted walnuts (optional)

♦ Extra walnuts for garnish (optional)

Cream Cheese Frosting

♦ 4 oz [113 g] cream cheese, room temperature

♦ 4 tablespoons [56 g] salted butter, room temperature

♦ 2 tablespoons [30 ml] pure maple syrup

♦ 2 teaspoons [10 ml] pure vanilla or rum

Makes one 9x13-inch [23x33-cm] cake

YERBA MATE BANANA SNACK CAKE

Preheat oven to 325 F [163 C]. Grease and line an 8x8-inch [20x20-cm] baking pan with parchment paper, overhanging sides for easy removal of cake; set aside.

CAKE

In a medium bowl, beat the banana, sugar, oil, eggs, vanilla, and sour cream with an electric mixer until thoroughly combined. In a large bowl, whisk together the flours, arrowroot, tea, baking soda, and sea salt. Add banana mixture to the dry ingredients; stir until fully incorporated.

Pour batter into prepared pan. Bake for 40-45 minutes until cake center springs back to the touch and tester comes out clean. Remove pan from oven to wire rack. Cool for 20 minutes. Lift cake out of pan with parchment paper handles. Allow to cool completely.

FROSTING

Beat the cream cheese with an electric mixer until light and fluffy. Stir in yogurt, vanilla, and confectioner's sugar. Beat until smooth and fluffy.

EnJOY!

INGREDIENTS

Cake

- 6 oz [170 g] mashed, ripe banana
- 3½ oz [100 g] coconut or brown sugar
- ¼ cup [60 ml] avocado or melted coconut oil
- 2 pastured eggs, room temperature
- ¼ cup [60 ml] sour cream or plain yogurt of choice
- 2 teaspoons [10 ml] pure vanilla or spiced rum
- 6 oz [170 g] almond flour
- 1 oz [28 g] GF flour blend or arrowroot powder
- 1 tablespoon [15 ml] dry Yerba mate tea, finely ground and strained through a sieve
- ½ teaspoon [2.5 ml] baking soda
- ¼ teaspoon [1.25 ml] sea salt

Yogurt-Cream Cheese Frosting

- 4 oz [113 g] cream cheese, room temperature
- ½ cup [120 ml] plain Greek yogurt
- 2 teaspoons [10 ml] pure vanilla
- 2 tablespoons [30 ml] confectioner's sugar

Makes one 8-inch [20-cm] cake

PIES, PASTRIES, & DESSERTS

homemade pie can be the talk of generations

Lemon Thyme Lemon Tart, 201

Coconut Banana Cream Pie, 203

Balsamic Strawberry Tarts, 205

Creamy Key Lime Cheesecake, 209

Blueberry-Basil Mascarpone Cheesecake, 211

Fudgy Pudding Cake, 213

Lemon Pudding Cake, 215

Grandma's Updated Apple Dumplings, 217

Pistachio-Rose Rice Pudding, 219

LEMON THYME LEMON TART

PASTRY

In the bowl of a food processor with attached blade, combine GF flour blend, sea salt, and sugars. Pulse to blend. Add butter pieces and pulse until well-incorporated. Add egg yolk and ice water 1 teaspoon at a time, pulsing until dough forms.

Turn tart dough onto one of the pieces of parchment paper. Gather dough to make disc shape. Top with remaining parchment paper. Roll out to 12-inch [30-cm] circle. Place on large baking sheet and chill for 1 hour.

LEMON CURD

Whisk together juice, zest, sugar, and eggs in a 2-quart [2-liter] heavy saucepan. Stir in butter and cook over med-low heat, whisking continuously, until curd thickens and first bubbles appears on surface, about 6 minutes. Transfer lemon curd to a bowl, cover and chill, until cold, at least 1 hour.

ASSEMBLE

Preheat oven to 375 F [190 C] Remove tart dough from refrigerator and allow to rest 5-10 minutes. Remove top parchment and invert the rolled dough into tart pan. Press dough to fill pan, adjusting as necessary. Cover with beeswax cloth, parchment, or a towel and freeze for 15 minutes. Place tart on baking sheet and bake for 25 minutes. Cool completely on wire rack before filling.

With an offset spatula, spread lemon curd over cooled pastry. Sprinkle lemon thyme leaves over curd. Top with whipped cream and fresh berries as desired.

EnJOY!

Makes one 10– or 11-inch [25-cm] tart

INGREDIENTS

Pastry

- 7 oz [198 g] GF flour blend
- ¼ teaspoon [1.25 ml] sea salt
- 1½ oz [43 g] dark brown sugar or coconut sugar
- 1 oz [28 g] confectioner's sugar
- ½ oz [14 g] unsweetened shredded coconut
- ½ cup [113 g] unsalted butter, roughly chopped and frozen
- 1 pastured egg yolk
- 1 teaspoon [5 ml] pure vanilla extract
- 2-4 [10-20 ml] teaspoons ice water
- 2 12-inch [30.5-cm] pieces of parchment paper
- 10 or 11-inch [25-28 cm] tart pan with removable bottom

Lemon Curd

- 2 teaspoons [10 ml] finely chopped fresh lemon zest
- ½ cup [120 ml] fresh lemon juice
- 3½ oz [100 g] granulated cane sugar
- 3 pastured eggs
- 6 tablespoons [85 g] unsalted butter, cut into small pieces
- 2 tablespoons [30 ml] fresh lemon thyme leaves

- Whipped cream (optional)
- Fresh berries (optional)

COCONUT BANANA CREAM PIE

CRUST

In the bowl of a food processor, combine GF flour, almond flour, coconut, baking powder, and sea salt. Pulse to blend well. Add frozen butter pieces and pulse until mixture looks like coarse crumbs. Add sour cream and pulse until dough begins to come together. If necessary, add 1-2 teaspoons [5-10 ml] of ice water. Turn dough into glass bowl, cover and freeze for 30 minutes.

Preheat oven to 400 F [204 C] and turn chilled dough onto a generously floured parchment-lined surface for rolling out. Sprinkle more flour over dough and roll into a 12-inch [30-cm] circle. Set a 10-inch [25-cm] glass pie plate upside down over dough, reach hand under parchment paper, and carefully flip dough into pie plate. Press dough into the plate and roll edges, crimping as desired and trimming where needed. Bake for 20-25 minutes until nicely golden. Cool completely.

FILLING

Combine 1 cup [240 ml] cream, 3 tablespoons [45 ml] sugar, and rum in a medium saucepan. Bring just to a simmer over medium heat. Do NOT boil. Remove from heat.

In a medium bowl, whisk yolks, remaining 3 tablespoons [45 ml] sugar, cornstarch and vanilla together. Add remaining ¼ cup [60 ml] cream and whisk until smooth.

Add about ¼ cup [60 ml] hot cream mixture to the egg mixture while whisking continually. Repeat with another ¼ cup hot cream, then whisk the egg mixture into the pan of hot cream on the stove. Set over medium heat and bring to a boil; stirring constantly. Boil 1-2 minutes, stirring constantly to prevent scorching, until thickened. Remove from heat, add cream cheese, and whisk until smooth.

Spread some filling over the bottom of the crust. Top with sliced bananas and cover bananas with remaining filling. Chill 1 hour. Top with slightly sweetened vanilla whipped cream and toasted unsweetened coconut as desired.

EnJOY!

INGREDIENTS

Crust

- 4 oz [113 g] GF flour blend, plus more for rolling pastry
- 3 oz [85 g] almond flour or GF flour blend
- ½ oz [14 g] shredded unsweetened coconut
- ¼ teaspoon [1.25 ml] baking powder
- ½ teaspoon [2.5 ml] sea salt
- 6 tablespoons [84 g] unsalted butter, roughly chopped and frozen
- ⅓ cup [80 g] full-fat sour cream, cold

Filling

- 1¼ cups [300 ml] heavy cream, divided
- 6 tablespoons [75 g] refined or unrefined cane sugar, divided
- 3 tablespoons [23 g] cornstarch or arrowroot powder
- 1 tablespoon [15 ml] spiced rum (optional)
- 2 teaspoons [10 ml] pure vanilla
- 5 pastured egg yolks
- 4 oz [113 g] cream cheese, cubed at room temperature
- 3 firm yellow bananas

- Vanilla whipped cream (optional)
- Toasted, unsweetened coconut (optional)

Makes one 10-inch [25-cm] pie

BALSAMIC STRAWBERRY TARTS

Preheat oven to 375 F [190 C].

CRUST

In a food processor, combine the flours, psyllium husk powder, baking powder, and sea salt. Pulse until mixed well. Add the butter and pulse until the mixture resembles coarse meal. Add the sour cream. Pulse until dough comes together. Scoop dough into a glass bowl; cover, and freeze for 30 minutes.

Sprinkle a parchment-lined surface with almond flour. Divide chilled dough into 4 equal pieces. Roll out each piece of dough to 5-inch [12-cm] circles on the parchment paper, sprinkling dough with additional almond flour as needed. Transfer rounds to four 4-inch [10-cm] tart pans, pressing in and crimping edges as desired.

FILLING

For the tart filling, in a medium bowl, combine strawberries, sugar, balsamic vinegar, melted butter, cornstarch, rosemary (or other herbs), and sea salt. Gently stir to combine. Divide filling between the four crusts. Lightly brush the edges of the tarts with the beaten egg white. Bake for about 40 minutes until edges are golden brown and filling is bubbly. Cool. Serve with whipped cream as desired.

EnJOY!

INGREDIENTS

Crust

- 3 oz [85 g] almond flour
- ½ oz [14 g] green plantain flour or GF flour blend
- ½ oz [14 g] tapioca flour
- ¼ teaspoon [1.25 ml] psyllium husk powder
- ¼ teaspoon [1.25 ml] baking powder
- ¼ teaspoon [1.25 ml] sea salt
- 4 tablespoons [56 g] unsalted butter, cold, cut into ½-inch pieces
- 3 tablespoons [45 ml] sour cream or plain yogurt of choice

Filling

- 10 oz [283 g] fresh strawberries, sliced
- 2 oz [56 g] refined or unrefined cane or coconut sugar
- 1-2 teaspoons [5-10 ml] best-quality aged balsamic vinegar or fresh lemon juice
- 1 tablespoon [14 g] unsalted butter, melted
- ½ teaspoon [2.5 ml] cornstarch, arrowroot or tapioca powder
- 2 teaspoons [10 ml] fresh rosemary, lemon thyme or basil, minced
- 2 pinches sea salt
- 1 pastured egg white, slightly beaten
- whipped cream (optional)

Makes four 4-inch [10-cm] tarts

FEAST AND GATHER, NEVADA CITY, CALIFORNIA

Meet Shanan Manuel. She is the inspiration, vision, and bone-tiring work behind Nevada City, California's Feast and Gather. You may think Feast and Gather is a farm-to-table restaurant or café. Nope. Shanan is a farm-to-table caterer and magical event-maker. Her ethos of "no anger in the kitchen," and "I can't do this without a team," has led her, and the culinary professionals who work with her, to adopt an iron-clad responsibility to the community they serve.

Feast and Gather believes that culinary professionals not only need the commitment of providing exceptional quality and service, but also the honesty in providing education about the effects our choices have on our bodies and the planet. Shanan demonstrates her unwavering integrity to her mission by designing each menu around what is seasonally available from local, organic, and grass-fed, free-range farmers.

Besides being the chef behind Nevada City's Farm-to-Table Dinner (where 150 diners enjoy a farm-sourced, six-course meal at one long table in downtown Nevada City, Shanan offers blindfolded dinner parties. She says that eating blindfolded opens up trust and unique experiences in "listening to your body." This has led to breakthrough healing, especially for those suffering with eating disorders.

Her mantra: "I can't care what other people think of me. I care." *Care she does—and it shows!*

CREAMY KEY LIME CHEESECAKE

CRUST

Preheat oven to 375 F [190 C]. In a 9- or 10-inch [22-25-cm] springform pan, combine crumbs, melted butter, and sugar. Press evenly over bottom of pan and halfway up sides. Bake 7 minutes.

FILLING

In a large mixing bowl with an electric mixer or in a stand mixer, beat cream cheese until fluffy. Add sugar; beat well, scraping sides and bottom of bowl frequently. Add sour cream, eggs, flour, and vanilla or rum; beat until smooth. Stir in lime juice.

Pour cheesecake filling over prepared crust. Return to 375 F [190 C] oven for 15 minutes. Lower temperature to 250 F [121 C] and continue baking 50 minutes for 10-inch [25-cm] pan, 55 minutes for 9-inch [22-cm] pan. Cool cheesecake in pan on wire rack for 20 minutes. Run a sharp knife around edge to loosen cheesecake crust, but do not remove from pan. Cool 1 hour more.

Refrigerate at least 6 hours before serving. Garnish with sweetened whipped cream, lime zest, or both as desired.

EnJOY!

INGREDIENTS

Crust

♦ 10 oz [284 g] GF graham crackers or oat grahams, ground into crumbs (a food processor works well)

♦ ½ cup [113 g] butter, ghee or coconut oil, melted

♦ 1½ oz [45 g] cane or coconut sugar

Filling

♦ 3 8-oz [228 g] packages of cream cheese (dairy or almond milk) at room temperature

♦ 7 oz [198 g] cane sugar or monk fruit sweetener

♦ 8 oz [228 g] sour cream or plain greek yogurt (or dairy-free alternative) at room temperature

♦ 1¼ oz [35 g] white rice flour or GF flour blend

♦ 4 pastured eggs at room temperature

♦ 2 teaspoons [10 ml] pure vanilla or rum

♦ ½ cup [120 ml] key lime juice or regular lime juice (or combination)

Lightly sweetened whipped cream (dairy or coconut) and lime zest for garnishing (optional).

Makes 12 servings

EVERYWHERE IS LOCAL

BLUEBERRY-BASIL
MASCARPONE CHEESECAKE

Preheat oven 350 F [176 C]. Tightly wrap the outside of a 10-inch [25-cm] springform pan with 3 layers of recycled heavy-duty recycled aluminum foil.

CRUST

Combine nuts, flour and sugar in the bowl of a food processor. Process the nuts until they are a fine meal. Add melted butter and pulse a few times until incorporated. Pour the crust mixture into the prepared springform pan and press to form an even layer over the bottom. Bake 10-12 minutes. Remove springform pan from the oven to a large roasting pan. Decrease the oven temperature to 325 F [162 C].

CHEESECAKE

Using an electric or stand mixer (with paddle attachment), beat the cream cheese, mascarpone, and sugar in a large bowl until smooth, scraping bowl occasionally with a rubber spatula. Beat in the lemon juice and vanilla. Add the eggs, one at a time, beating just until blended after each addition. Pour the cheese mixture over the crust in the pan. Pour enough hot water into the roasting pan to come halfway up the sides of the springform pan. Bake until the center of the cheesecake jiggles slightly when the pan is gently shaken, about 60-65 minutes. Transfer the cheesecake to a cooling rack for 1 hour. Refrigerate for at least 8-48 hours.

TOPPING

In a small saucepan, combine sugar and cornstarch. Stir in cold water, lemon juice, and blueberries. Turn heat to medium. and bring to a boil, stirring continuously. Cook an additional 3-4 minutes until thickened. Remove from heat, add fresh basil, and allow to cool. Pour cooled topping on cheesecake before serving.

EnJOY!

Makes one 10-inch [25-cm] cheesecake

INGREDIENTS

Crust

- 1½ cups [188 g] walnut or pecan halves
- ½ cup [60 g] GF flour blend
- 2 tablespoons [30 ml] unrefined or refined cane sugar, coconut sugar or monk fruit
- 4 tablespoons [56 g] salted butter, melted

Cheesecake

- 2 8-oz [113 g] packages cream cheese, room temperature
- 1 16-oz [454 g] container mascarpone cheese, room temperature
- 1¼ cups [250 g] cane sugar, coconut sugar, or monk fruit (or combination)
- 1 tablespoon [15 ml] fresh lemon juice
- 2 teaspoons [10 ml] pure vanilla
- 4 pastured eggs, room temperature
- Hot water

Topping

- ¼ cup [50 g] cane sugar, coconut sugar or monk fruit
- 2 tablespoons [16 g] cornstarch, tapioca, or arrowroot powder
- ½ cup [120 ml] cold water
- 2 tablespoons [30 ml] fresh lemon juice
- 2 cups [480 ml] fresh (or frozen) blueberries
- 1-2 tablespoons [15-30 ml] fresh basil, finely julienned

EVERYWHERE IS LOCAL

FUDGY PUDDING CAKE

Preheat oven to 400 F [204 C]. Fill a small saucepan with 1-inch [2.5 cm] of water. Place a larger stainless steel or glass bowl on top of the pan to make a double boiler. Turn heat to medium-high.

Add the chocolate and butter to the bowl sitting on the pan of simmering water. Whisk the chocolate and butter, as it quickly melts, until nearly completely smooth. Turn off the heat and add the sugar and vanilla. Continue to whisk the chocolate until completely smooth.

Carefully remove the bowl from the hot pan to the counter. Allow the chocolate to cool for 5 minutes, stirring occasionally. When the 5 minutes are up, slowly drizzle the egg into the chocolate mixture, whisking vigorously and continuously to prevent the egg from cooking. Continue to do this until the chocolate batter looks smooth. Stir in the flour until smooth again

Generously spray or butter the bottom and sides of one 4-8-oz [120-240-ml] ramekin or coffee mug. Pour the batter into the ramekin and place on a baking sheet. Bake for 10-12 minutes. The cake should appear to be baked but when touched in the center will feel very soft.

Remove the cake from the oven and allow it rest for a minute. This dessert can be served in the ramekin or flipped over onto a plate. If flipping, slide a knife around the inside of the ramekin to make sure nothing is sticking. Cover the ramekin with a serving plate and flip the plate to right side up. Slowly and carefully begin to lift the ramekin off the plate.

Dust the fudge pudding cake with powdered sugar if desired and/or dollop with a small spoonful of dairy or non-dairy whipped cream or ice cream flavor of choice.

EnJOY!

INGREDIENTS

- 1 oz [28 g] semi-sweet or dark chocolate chips or chopped chocolate of choice
- 2 tablespoons [28 g] butter, ghee, or vegan butter alternative
- ¼ oz [7 g] coconut sugar, cane sugar, or monk fruit sweetener
- ¼ teaspoon [1.25 ml] vanilla, rum, almond liqueur, orange liqueur, hazelnut liqueur, or raspberry liqueur
- 1 pastured egg, room temperature, well beaten
- ¼ oz [7 g] almond flour or GF flour blend

Makes one serving (multiply ingredients as needed for desired number of servings)

EVERYWHERE IS LOCAL

LEMON PUDDING CAKE

Preheat oven to 325 F [163 C] . Butter four-8 oz [240 ml] ramekins; set aside in large baking dish.

In a medium bowl, beat egg yolks, buttermilk, lemon juice, and lemon zest until well combined. Reduce the speed to low and blend in flour, sugar, and sea salt. In a separate bowl with clean beaters, beat egg whites until stiff peaks form. Fold egg whites into egg yolk mixture with a rubber spatula. Divide batter evenly between ramekins. Pour hot water into the baking pan, halfway up sides of ramekins.

Bake for 45 minutes until golden and the tops of the cakes spring back when gently pressed. Allow to cool slightly, then carefully invert cakes onto plates. Serve with fresh berries and dust with powdered sugar.

EnJOY!

INGREDIENTS

- 1 tablespoon [14 g] unsalted butter
- 3 oz [85 g] superfine or confectioner's sugar, plus more for dusting
- 2 pastured eggs, separated
- ⅔ cup [160 ml] buttermilk, whole milk, or full-fat coconut milk
- 3 tablespoons [45 ml] fresh lemon juice
- 1 tablespoon [15 ml] lemon zest, finely chopped
- 1 oz [28 g] GF flour blend
- ¼ teaspoon [1.25 ml] sea salt
- Boiling water
- Fresh berries

Makes 4 servings

GRANDMA'S UPDATED APPLE DUMPLINGS

This recipe is an adaptation of a 100+-year-old family favorite passed down from my grandmother. I have fond memories of Sunday dinner at Grandma's when a big pan of apple dumplings would be on the counter when we came over, and the time she taught me how to make them as a newlywed, and when I then made them for my children.

Preheat oven to 400 F [204 C] and butter a 9x13-inch [23x33-cm] glass baking dish; set aside.

DUMPLINGS

Mix flours, sugar, and baking powder in the bowl of a food processor. Pulse to blend. Add butter and cream cheese. Pulse until mixture looks like coarse crumbs. Pour in buttermilk and pulse until dough comes together in big chunks. Turn dough onto a generously floured surface and sprinkle with additional GF flour. Roll out to ¼-inch [6-mm] thickness. With knife, score dough to make 8 squares (they do not have to be perfect).

In a small bowl, combine 1 oz [28 g] sugar, cinnamon, and nutmeg. Peel, core, and slice or quarter apples. (If using apple slices, dumplings will bake flatter.) Divide apples between dough sections. Dot with butter and sprinkle apples with sugar -spice mixture. Using a metal spatula to assist, gather up dough around apple mound, pinching seams together and molding into a somewhat rounded shape. Place each dumpling seam-side down in prepared dish.

SAUCE

Combine sugars, cornstarch, cinnamon and nutmeg in a saucepan. Slowly pour in cold water, stirring constantly. Add butter. Stir over medium heat until mixture boils. Cook and stir 1 minute. Remove from heat

Option 1) Pour some sauce around dumplings before baking. Leave at least half the sauce for serving after.

Option 2) Bake dumplings without sauce.

Bake dumplings at 400 F [204 C] for 10 minutes. Reduce heat to 350 F [176 C] and bake an additional 25 minutes. Serve with warm sauce.

EnJOY!

INGREDIENTS

Dumplings

- 8 oz [226 g] GF flour blend
- 1 oz [28 g] almond flour
- 1 tablespoon [15 ml] refined or unrefined cane sugar
- 2 teaspoons [10 ml] baking powder
- 12 tablespoons [160 g] cold salted butter, cut up
- 4 tablespoons [56 g] cream cheese, cut up
- ¾ cup [180 ml] buttermilk or milk of choice
- 3-4 cooking apples (such as McIntosh, Cortland, Jonathan, or Honeycrisp)
- 1 oz refined or unrefined cane sugar, coconut sugar, or maple sugar
- 1 teaspoon [5 ml] Ceylon cinnamon
- ¼ teaspoon [1.25 ml] ground nutmeg
- 2 tablespoons [28 g] butter, cut into 8 pieces

Sauce

- 7 oz [198 g] refined or unrefined cane sugar
- 2 oz [56 g] brown sugar, coconut sugar, or maple sugar
- 4 tablespoons [60 ml] cornstarch or tapioca flour
- 4 teaspoons [20 ml] Ceylon cinnamon
- ½ teaspoon [2.5 ml] ground nutmeg
- 3½ cups [840 ml] cold water
- ½ cup [56 g] salted butter

Makes eight servings

PISTACHIO-ROSE RICE PUDDING

Cook the rice with canned coconut milk according to package instructions.

Mix the cooked rice, 1½ cups [360 ml] milk of choice, sugar, and sea salt. In a medium saucepan, cook uncovered over medium-low heat for 15-20 minutes; stirring frequently. Meanwhile, heat a dry frying pan to medium heat, and toast the pistachios until aromatic, 3-5 minutes

Whisk egg and remaining milk of choice in a 2-cup [480-ml] glass measure. Add about 1 cup [240 ml] of the hot rice mixture to the egg while stirring continuously. Stir the egg-rice mixture back into the rice on the stove. Cook 2 minutes; stirring frequently.

Remove from heat and stir in butter (ghee or coconut oil) rosewater, and vanilla. Serve warm, room temperature or cold. Garnish with toasted pistachios and rose petals.

EnJOY!

PISTACHIO MILK

Line a fine-meshed sieve with a double layer of cheese-cloth and set it over an 8-cup [2-liter] glass measure. Drain pistachios. Combine pistachios and hot water in blender. Blend on high for 2-3 minutes. Carefully pour blended nuts through cheesecloth-lined sieve; gather cheesecloth together and squeeze out remaining liquid (ground pistachi-os can be used as an almond flour replacement in cakes and muffins)

Add maple syrup, sea salt, cardamom, and vanilla to pistachio milk and whisk together. Cool completely, then transfer to a bottle or jar and store in the refrigerator for up to one week.

INGREDIENTS

♦ 1 cup [197 g] uncooked Arborio rice

♦ 1 13.5-oz [398 ml] can fair-trade, unsweetened coconut milk

♦ 2 cups [480 ml] milk (pistachio milk-*see below*, coconut milk, or equal parts whole milk & cream), divided

♦ ⅓ cup [80 ml] unrefined or refined cane sugar [67 g] or pure maple syrup

♦ Pinch sea salt

♦ 1 pastured duck egg or extra-large pastured chicken egg

♦ 1 tablespoon [14 g] butter, ghee, or coconut oil [15 ml]

♦ 1-2 tablespoons [15-30 ml] rosewater

♦ ½ teaspoon [2.5 ml] pure vanilla or pure vanilla powder

♦ ½ cup [120 ml] toasted pistachios, very finely chopped

♦ Edible rose petals for garnish

Pistachio Milk (if using)

♦ 1 cup [240 ml] raw shelled pistachios, covered with water by 2 inches, soaked overnight

♦ 4 cups [1 liter] hot (not boiling) water

♦ 2 tablespoons [30 ml] pure maple syrup or golden syrup

♦ ¼ teaspoon [1.25 ml] sea salt

♦ ¼ teaspoon [1.25 ml] freshly ground cardamom

♦ ½ teaspoon [2.5 ml] pure vanilla

Makes 4—6 servings

INDEX

RECIPES: BREADS, MUFFINS & PANCAKES

RECIPES: CAKES, PIES, & PASTRY